London on Film

100 years of filmmaking in London

First published in Great Britain in 1996
by the Museum of London,
150 London Wall, London EC2Y 5HN

Copyright © Museum of London 1996

British Library Cataloguing-in-Publication Data

A CIP catalogue record for this book is
available from the British Library

ISBN 0 904818 65 9

Printed and bound in Great Britain by
The White Dove Press

Project Manager: Suzie Burt
Design: Vicky Fullick
Editorial: Zelda Baveystock, Suzie Burt, Rachel Daley,
Doreen Palamartschuk

London on Film

100 years of filmmaking in London **Colin Sorensen**

museum of
LONDON

Contents

Acknowledgements 6

Foreword 7

Preface 8

Introduction 9

Forerunners 13

The Arrival of British Movies 17

London on Film

POLITICS 27

TIME FOR CHANGE 34

WAR 40

ON THE MOVE 43

Londoners

SOCIAL CONTRASTS 51

WORK AND PLAY 56

THE STREET, THE MARKET,
   THE CLUB AND THE PUB 66

THE CHILD ALONE 75

POP HEROES AS VILLAINS 76

The Story of the Studios

FLICKER ALLEY 79

ROLL OF HONOUR 82

A CENTURY OF STUDIOS 83

INTERVIEW WITH SIDNEY COLE 86

LIFE IN THE STUDIOS 90

INTERVIEW WITH ERNIE DIAMOND 92

London Locations

THE ART DEPARTMENT 97

THE BACKLOT 106

ON LOCATION 110

DRESSED FOR THE PART 112

INTERVIEW WITH ASSHETON GORTON 115

LOST LONDON I 119

LOST LONDON II – THE BOMBED CITY 121

LOCATION AS ACTOR 123

POINTS OF CONVERGENCE 128

BRIDGES AND THEATRES 132

INTERVIEW WITH DOUGLAS SLOCOMBE 136

Past and Future, Myth and Legend

RECREATING THE PAST 141

PROPHESYING THE FUTURE 145

MYTH AND LEGEND 148

AS OTHERS SEE US 152

INTERVIEW WITH KEVIN BROWNLOW 156

INTERVIEW WITH PATRICK KEILLER 160

INTERVIEW WITH ROY BOULTING 162

List of illustrations 166

Acknowledgements

The idea that the Museum of London should celebrate the centenary of the movies in Britain evolved out of the 'Made in London' film seasons (a joint enterprise between the Museum and the National Film and Television Archive), that have been a popular fixture at the Museum for sixteen years. It was agreed that I should, as a curatorial swan-song, research and organise an exhibition exploring London's place in the story of the movies. To Max Hebditch, the Director of the Museum of London, my thanks therefore for the opportunity to fulfil a long-held ambition. My gratitude also to David Francis, previously Curator of the National Film and Television Archive (now Chief of the Motion Picture, Broadcasting, and Recorded Sound Division of the Library of Congress, Washington DC.) and to Clyde Jeavons, his successor and to Anne Fleming, the Deputy Curator for their enthusiastic help and the unprecedented access they allowed me to the treasures in their care. To their colleagues in London and the J. Paul Getty Conservation Centre at Berkhamsted and, in particular to Luke McKernan, Frank Holland, Elaine Burrows, Bridget Kinally, Jane Hockings, Henning Schou, David Peterson, June Elvey, Don Geary and Maureen Edmonds, I am forever indebted.

From the many distinguished past and present members of the film industry with whom I have been privileged to discuss the project, I have derived much instruction and assistance. Lord Attenborough very kindly contributed to our initial sponsorship brochure and has written a foreword to this publication. Lack of space prevents me from particularising, but my thanks go warmly to Ken Adam, Christabel Albery, Roy Boulting, Kevin Brownlow, Maurice Carter, Diana Charnley, Sidney Cole, Stuart Craig, Daniel Dark, Nick Daubeny, Ernie Diamond, Harvey Edgington, Christine Edzard, Harry Elam, Richard Goodwin, Assheton Gorton, Philippe Hartman, Diana Hawkins, Patrick Keiller, Gavin Millar, Sydney Samuelson, Anthony Simmons, Douglas Slocombe, Olivier Stockman and Alan Tompkins. To the many film distributors and copyright owners who have helped, I would like to extend my grateful thanks.

My erstwhile colleagues in the Museum of London's Photographic Department – Barrington Gray, Torla Evans, John Chase and Richard Stroud – coped cheerfully with the considerable load I placed upon them. At the Theatre Museum Dr James Fowler and Barry Norman hunted for evidence, as did David Cheshire at the Theatres Trust, and Graeme Cruikshank in the Palace Theatre Archives. Stephen Bourne and Denis Gifford kindly searched their files. At the Local History collections at Hammersmith (Christine Bayliss) and Haringey (Rita Read) I found valuable illustrations. I was accorded much generous assistance by many friends and fellow enthusiasts including: Elizabeth LeBas, Professor David Mayer, Professor Christopher Baugh, Richard Doust, Donald Rumbelow, Tim Brown, Richard Mangan of the Mander and Mitchenson Collection, Michelle Aubert of Le Centre National de la Cinématographie, Bois d'Arcy and the staff of the Motion Picture, Broadcasting, and Recorded Sound Division of the Library of Congress, Washington DC., Chris Mohr's confidence and textual acuity were invaluable. Zelda Baveystock, Suzie Burt and Vicky Fullick of the Museum's Publications Department had the unenviable task of selecting and re-ordering exhibition material to accommodate it in this publication. To my wife Mary (Lovat) and my daughter, Clare, my apologies for more than two years of severe domestic disruption.

Lastly, I must thank my 'team'. Liz Heasman is surely the best and most experienced researcher in the business. Kate Boulting regularly and conscientiously created order out of chaos, and to Rachel Daley I owe a huge debt of gratitude for her meticulous work and stalwart, zealous support. Without her help this project could not have been accomplished.

Colin Sorensen, Keeper Emeritus, Museum of London

Foreword

Few of the Victorians who, in the late 1890s, paid to see London's first presentations of 'Animated Photographs' could have imagined that, within a few years, this intriguing scientific toy would become one of the city's major industries and the twentieth century's new art of record and imagination.

During 1995–96 there will be many events to celebrate cinema's hundred years of achievement and undoubtedly the *London on Film* exhibition, revealing the many ways in which the history of our capital has interacted with moving pictures, is one of the most fascinating.

As a former Chairman of the British Film Institute, it gives me particular pleasure that this exhibition, mounted by the Museum of London, has drawn upon the unrivalled collection of indigenous films preserved at the Institute's National Film and Television Archive.

This uniquely rich resource will not only help to reveal the documentary facts of city life over the past hundred years, but also vividly demonstrates how succeeding generations of filmmakers have entertained cinema audiences with fictional ideas and stories about London's past, present and future.

Lord Attenborough of Richmond-upon-Thames, Chairman, National Council of Cinema 100

Preface

When, in 1935, the British Film Institute created what is now the National Film and Television Archive, its founding curator, Ernest Lindgren, made a visionary decision. Rather than regard films exclusively (and, at the time, fashionably) as examples of the new art form of the twentieth century and choose to preserve them only on that basis, he recognised their unique and wide-ranging value as dynamic records of contemporary life and behaviour – the first time a century's social history had been captured in moving pictures.

In contrast to every other burgeoning film archive and cinémathèque of the day, Lindgren thus gave equal priority and weight to the collecting of all categories of film – fiction and non-fiction, narrative and documentary – as carriers of visual evidence of our life and times. Cinema could be art, but film, he said, was 'living history'.

Lindgren and the BFI thereby stimulated the serious use of film as an historical and educational tool, although traditional historians were notoriously slow to see it as anything other than unreliable, ephemeral 'wallpaper':

too often it proved their cherished speculations wrong! Even now, there are those who treat film (often with wanton inaccuracy) as mere illustration to leaven a thesis, rather than as a vital, primary document in its own right.

Colin Sorensen and the Museum of London stand as shining exceptions, having long confounded the carpetbaggers of contemporary historical study by taking film, in all its guises, real or false, as seriously as any other document or artefact in revealing – and freezing in time – their essential subject-matter: the social, archaeological and pictorial history of London.

As Colin Sorensen says, the British feature film – whether it be *Oliver Twist, Seven Days to Noon* or a *Crazy Gang* romp – is as much about London as any deliberate documentary record of the city itself, and his trust in the NFTVA's vast collection in pursuing this theme so compellingly, alone justifies the eclectic selection and preservation policy handed down to us by Ernest Lindgren.

London on Film is a brilliant concept and an entirely appropriate contribution to the British

centenary of cinema celebrations. It is also a richly satisfying culmination of work-in-progress in the sixteen year collaboration between the Museum of London and the BFI's Archive which will both strengthen and fuel the continuing research. Dr Johnson said, 'When a man is tired of London, he is tired of life.' We feel the same way about movies.

Clyde Jeavons
Curator, National Film and Television
Archive, British Film Institute

Introduction

London on Film has been created for the Museum of London in close association with the National Film and Television Archive, a division of the British Film Institute. It is presented as one of the celebrations that have been arranged all over the country to commemorate the centenary of the 'movies' in Britain – that is to say, the first public screening of motion pictures before a paying audience. The project has been planned with complementary purposes: to explore not only the historical record but also the influence of London on film and the influence of film on London.

Luke McKernan's chapter on page 17 recounts with admirable clarity the events surrounding the arrival of projected motion pictures in London. Since then a vast amount of information recording the life and times of London has been accumulated on film – not only in those non-fiction or documentary films which have sought to explore the factual, but also in the thousands of fiction films which have used London as their setting. This unique accumulation of insight and information, of fact and fantasy, has created a vast resource for the study and appreciation of London. It offers us a largely unprobed field for a new kind of urban archaeology: the archaeology of recorded action rather than of surviving artefact. However, we need to remember that whereas an historically significant object may survive buried in the ground for centuries, film is all too fragile and vulnerable. For over half of the century of filmmaking we are now celebrating, this unique medium of record was fatally flawed. All film produced on 35mm stock before 1951 was printed on a chemically unstable nitrate base. This was not only highly flammable but subject to inevitable deterioration, resulting ultimately in its decomposition into a useless sticky mass.

It now seems astonishing how indifferent and careless was the general attitude to old film, not only on the part of the producers and exhibitors who, once it had passed its useful commercial life, usually consigned a film to the flames, but on the part of those who might have been expected to recognise the creative or historical significance of what had been filmed. In this country it was not until 1935 that the National Film Library (as it was then known) was established as a part of the British Film Institute to 'preserve the art of the film'. We should here pay homage to Ernest Lindgren, its first curator, who pioneered this immense task – a task by no means complete. To rescue the achievements of half a century it is now necessary to copy everything that survives onto more stable, safety acetate film. An immense and costly undertaking, the implications of which are all too little appreciated for the historical documentation of our century.

The first motion pictures were thought of as a fascinating optical curiosity. Almost immediately, however, film found a wider audience in the music halls. Having evolved during the 1840s and 1850s from late-night song rooms and taverns, music hall had, by the 1890s, become London's most successful form of popular entertainment, providing a wide variety of attractions. Jugglers, acrobats, ballets, short dramatic plays and, above all, comic singers, made up the bill at well over fifty halls in and around London. Always on the look out for additional attractions, the music hall managers immediately recognised the potential of the *Cinématographe* and its rival devices and quickly installed them. By the end of 1896, most of London's leading music halls included films in their programmes. Among the first to do so were the rival Empire and Alhambra Theatres of Varieties in Leicester Square.

A Lumière *Cinématographe* programme was to be seen at the Empire, and at the Alhambra R W Paul was even given facilities to make films on the roof that were then shown downstairs in the theatre. This small rooftop installation above Leicester Square was thus among the very earliest of London's film studios.

Few at that time could have imagined how quickly the motion picture, like an infant cuckoo, would oust its host from the nest. By the end of the 1920s many central and suburban London music halls had been converted into cinemas. To supply them and the hundreds of purpose-built cinemas, special studios had been constructed or adapted from existing buildings. A new London entertainment industry had been born.

The story of London's film studios forms an important part of this book. Although relatively few people have ever been permitted to see 'behind the scenes', the London film industry has been from its outset a fascinating amalgam of new and old London skills. It inevitably drew much from the traditional skills of theatre, circus and music hall, but also gave employment to many other crafts and professions. Every day through the studio gates came architectural draughtsmen, carpenters, decorative plaster workers, electricians, plumbers and many others, to join the actors, costumiers, make-up artists, animal trainers and property masters. Now, a century after the arrival of the

Cinématographe, many of London's once-famous studios have disappeared. The archaeology of the art and technology of filmmaking in London must be pursued mainly in the films themselves, and in the recollections of those who worked in the industry.

If there is a single subject or setting that can be said to characterise or predominate in British films it is that of London itself. The city has been the chosen location so often that one might reasonably identify these films as 'Londons' in the same way one talks of 'Westerns'. For this reason it is appropriate that the exhibition that this book accompanies is presented at the museum dedicated to telling the story of London. Just as Charles Dickens and other novelists and artists have invested London and its population with a sharply observed individuality, film has also explored and romanticised the city.

If *London on Film* has a bias in its choice of evidence, it must be admitted that much of the material has been chosen from the first half of the century. Not only does television increasingly predominate as the audio-visual chronicler as we approach our own time, but it has been frankly impossible to resist the temptation to explore the vanished London that can be revisited when looking at these earlier films. H G Wells published his first novel, *The Time Machine*, in 1895, the year in which the Lumière Brothers first demonstrated

...eir *Cinématographe* in Paris. Surely the motion picture camera and projector have proved to be the true time machines of our century.

At the age of twelve, I visited my first film studio, the one-time home of Korda's London Film Productions at Denham. Since then I have always been fascinated by opportunities to witness that unique combination of artistic and technological skill that characterises the processes of filmmaking. For twenty-five years I was a professional student of London history as Keeper of the Modern Department at the Museum of London. It has therefore been a particularly enjoyable exercise to bring together two of my most abiding interests. I am acutely aware, however, that I have only been scratching at the surface of this intriguing subject. The collaboration and support of my colleagues at the National Film and Television Archive – in particular Clyde Jeavons, Curator, and Anne Fleming, Deputy Curator – have encouraged me to believe that research will continue after the completion of the exhibition.

To return to my archaeological analogy, it has been important, indeed vital, to the range and detail of this project that I have been permitted to 'dig' for my evidence among the immense quantity of material preserved by the NFTVA. In particular, I have been able to make frame-enlargement photographs directly from films of which there had previously been no still images available.

Since the uniqueness of movies is that they move (or seem to), it may seem perverse to celebrate them in an exhibition and publication largely consisting of static images. Although, however, the exhibition does include numerous film extracts and is partnered by a lengthy season of cinema screenings, the purpose has been to stop the action, catch the gesture, freeze and examine the moment, and in so doing to add to our awareness of just how much there is recorded and preserved of London on film.

Colin Sorensen
Keeper Emeritus
Museum of London

Chapter one

Forerunners: Before the Pictures Began to Move

For centuries London has been one of the world's great centres of professional entertainment. London audiences were noted for their love of novelty, exciting dramatic action and magnificent spectacle.

Long before the coming of the 'movies', Londoners were familiar with many of the themes and techniques that were to be adopted by the film industry. They watched 'living newsreels' – re-enactments of recent events, and exotic presentations set in faraway countries, often including 'special effects' recreated on stage such as real waterfalls and live animals. Immense circular landscape paintings called panoramas were popular attractions, as were later full-scale recreations in wood, plaster and paint of such glamorous

The Times, 18 August 1789
Philip Astley, the reputed 'founding father' of the modern circus, presented thrilling demonstrations of trick horseriding and dramatic spectacle at his Amphitheatre, located at the southern end of Westminster Bridge. Encouraged by the Queen of France, Marie Antoinette, Astley opened a similar amphitheatre in Paris, where he was an eyewitness to the outbreak of the French Revolution. He presented a theatrical recreation of this event only four weeks later in London.

locations as Venice and Constantinople – film sets before films.

At the Diorama in Regent's Park, audiences seated in a darkened auditorium saw moving pictures, as a long painted canvas illuminated from behind was slowly unrolled to illustrate a narrator's adventures – a journey down the Nile, for example, or a visit to the wonders of the East. At the circus, audiences imagined a dramatic cross-country chase as gallant horsemen rode round the ring, leaping over various obstacles that were placed in their paths. Public pageants and street spectacles such as the Lord Mayor's Show and coronations were, along with military tournaments and recreations of battles, also a popular feature of London life.

The coming of the motion picture camera absorbed and transformed all these into the raw material of cinematic entertainment. The first flickering movies were seen as added attractions on the programme at the music halls: the form of entertainment most immediately affected by the coming of film and which, within a few years, would be largely replaced by it.

Sioux, Apache and Navajo Braves in the Red Man Spectacle, Earls Court

Far left: Earlier in the nineteenth century one of the regular night-time attractions at the Surrey Gardens had been a recreation of the Fire of London, making much use of smoke and flame. But London had never seen anything on such a scale as 'The Last Days of Pompeii', first produced by Paine's (the firework manufacturers) in 1896, in the grounds of Alexandra Palace. Each summer for fourteen years Londoners flocked to this immense presentation involving thousands of performers and elaborate sets which culminated in the eruption of Vesuvius.

Above left: 'Constantinople', Olympia, 1892
Visitors to Olympia in 1892 witnessed exotic scenes of oriental splendour in an elaborate evocation of this city, constructed on a special 'wide-screen' stage in the Main Hall.

Left: 'The Red Man Spectacle',
Earls Court, 1909
Imported Apache and Navajo braves gave authenticity to a spectacle which climaxed with a thrilling enactment of a massacre, staged around the log cabin of a white settler.

Chapter 2

The Arrival of British Movies

Luke McKernan, Historian, National Film and Television Archive

Moving pictures came to London and to Britain on 17 October 1894, in the form of the Edison Kinetoscope. This peepshow device showed its brief films on a loop to a single viewer. The location of the Kinetoscope parlour was 70 Oxford Street, and it was run by two Americans, Franck Z Maguire and Joseph D Baucus. On show were a dance from the voluptuous Carmencita, a cock fight, scenes in a bar room, a blacksmith's and a barber's shop, the serpentine dancer Annabelle and a wrestling match.

These films were all from America, produced at West Orange in Edison's Black Maria studio. British film production began when two Greek entrepreneurs, George Georgiades and George Tragides, having opened their own Kinetoscope

Robert W Paul with his camera.

parlours in London later that same year, approached a British electrical engineer of Hatton Garden, Robert W Paul, to construct further Kinetoscopes for them. Paul discovered that Edison had neglected to patent his moving picture invention in Britain, and at the further prompting of Georgiades and Tragides (who were certainly not acting as authentic Edison agents) Paul began to consider how he might make further films to show in these illicit Kinetoscopes.

Through a mutual acquaintance, Henry Short, Paul approached Birt Acres, a photographer and manager of the dry plate works of the firm Elliott & Son of Barnet. Together the two men constructed Britain's first moving picture camera between February and March 1895, and on 29 March Paul somewhat cheekily sent a strip to Thomas Edison from their very first film production. This was a short scene showing Henry Short in cricket whites (to show up better on the film) coming out of Acres' house, Clovelly Cottage, in Barnet.

Acres and Paul then went into serious film production the following day, when Acres filmed the Oxford and Cambridge Boat Race. Over the next three months, Acres and Paul produced the first British movies: *Carpenter's Shop, The Arrest of a Pickpocket, The Comic Shoeblack, The Boxing Kangaroo* and *The Derby,* amongst others. These then saw their debut at the Empire of India Exhibition, Earl's Court, where Paul's Kinetoscopes were on display from May until October 1895. By that time, however, the founding fathers of British film, incompatible as personalities, had gone their separate ways in a split that became acrimonious.

Below: A scene from what is believed to be the 1895 Derby, filmed by Birt Acres.

Right: From a lofty vantage point, Birt Acres (to the right of the camera) filmed the 1895 Derby.

Left: The Polytechnic in Regent Street, where the Lumière's *Cinématographe* was first shown to the London press on 20 February 1896.

Below: The cover for the programme of the first *Cinématographe* shows includes the name of Félicien Trewey, the entertainer and magician who presented the Lumière shows in London.

Right: The remarkable Egyptian Hall which once stood nearly opposite the Royal Academy in Piccadilly. Home to many wonders and curiosities, R W Paul's Theatrograph became an attraction there on 19 March 1896. The twin statues of *Isis* and *Osiris* now stand at the main entrance to the Museum of London.

Right: Within a few months, Paul had become London's leading filmmaker. He was engaged to supply regular items to be added to the bill at the famous Alhambra in Leicester Square, and other music halls.

In June 1895, following an invitation from a German business concern, Birt Acres went to Germany to film the opening of the Kiel Canal. On his return in July he found Paul now promoting himself solely, and the two broke up their business partnership and turned individually to further film production and the solution of projecting images on a screen, which had already been achieved in March 1895 by the Lumière brothers in France. Both men came up with the answers at roughly the same time, and with the triumphant public debut of the Lumière *Cinématographe* in Paris in December 1895 showing the great popularity of projected film, both sought to demonstrate their new machines as the Lumières were preparing to make their debut in England. Acres, who may have achieved some rudimentary projection late in 1895, was the first, when he presented a short programme of film with his Kinetic Camera to members of the Lyonsdown Photographic Club on 10 January 1896. This was presumably a dry run for his more prestigious appearance before members of the Royal Photographic Society at 12 Hanover Square on 14 January. These first

projected film shows in Britain were for private audiences only; similarly, Paul's first exhibition of his Theatrograph projector at Finsbury Technical College on 20 February 1896 was to a scientific audience, though he had considerable problems achieving any sort of adequate image on the screen.

But on the same day the Lumière *Cinématographe* had been given a press show at the Polytechnic in Regent Street, home of popular scientific lectures and displays. The host was magician and entertainer Félicien Trewey, and although the *Cinématographe* opened where it might gain approval as an interesting scientific novelty, the following day admission charges were made and a

race was on to bring moving pictures to the general public.

At this stage 'movies' were taken out of the hands of the inventors and into those of the showmen. Robert Paul made the transition with ease, Birt Acres did not. First to get to the West End was Félicien Trewey with the Lumière *Cinématographe*, which opened as an attraction in the variety bill of the Empire Leicester Square on 9 March. On 19 March Robert Paul's Theatrograph opened at the Egyptian Hall, Piccadilly, under the aegis of magician David Devant. Two days after Birt Acres' newly-named Kineoptikon opened at 2 Piccadilly Mansions, and on the same day Paul's Theatrograph was exhibited at Olympia. Renamed as the Animatographe, Paul's machine further opened at the Alhambra music hall on 25 March, where it was to enjoy a long residency.

Thus by March 1896 movies were established in London, and had already begun to spread out into the provinces. They had found their true homes, the variety theatres, which within only a few years would find this passing

Right: Paul's success prompted him to construct a more ambitious 'studio'. Built in North London near the Alexandra Palace at New Southgate, it took the form of a glass-roofed theatre where Paul could film short plays.

curiosity tucked at the end of the bill come to take over such theatres and bring to an end the golden age of the music hall. But in 1896 no one could have foreseen that moving pictures would become the dominant entertainment medium of the succeeding century. For some, the cinematograph was a novel invention, an extension of the art of photography, best exhibited to select groups. This was the route that Acres followed, exhibiting before royalty

on 21 July at Marlborough House and touring the country giving shows to photographic and scientific societies. He developed a small gauge camera for amateur use and remained close to his photographic roots.

Robert Paul, on the other hand, warmly adopted his new role as showman and the cinematograph's role as a public entertainer. Resuming film production in April 1896 he began making short story films, the first of

Just over a year after its first appearance in London, the cinematograph had a subject of worldwide interest to record. On 22 June 1897, Queen Victoria celebrated her Diamond Jubilee, commemorating her sixty years as Queen, with a magnificent thanksgiving ceremony in front of St Paul's Cathedral. Pioneer cameramen (R W Paul among them) assembled in force to record the event.

which, *The Soldier's Courtship*, was shot on the roof of the Alhambra. He scored a remarkable triumph when his film of the 1896 Derby, won by the Prince of Wales' Persimmon, was shown at the Alhambra and Canterbury the following evening, a coup which stunned its audience, who demanded that the film be shown over and over again. He retained his position at the forefront of the growing British film industry, establishing a studio and a laboratory, and sending cameramen out to film the important news stories of the day, notably Queen Victoria's Diamond Jubilee and the Boer War. Pioneers tend to see others profit from their innovations. Not so Paul, who remained a leading figure in the industry for over a dozen years before returning to his electrical work full-time.

Birt Acres, however, never found his place in the emergent moving picture entertainment business. Having, unlike Paul, given up his previous work to concentrate fully on films, he struggled on with his film and photographic work, though ceasing film production after 1900. Eventually made bankrupt, he failed to come to terms with the commercialisation of film. To invent moving pictures was not enough. Cinema – images not for private consumption but thrown upon a large screen for all to see – demanded an audience. And it was in the variety theatres of London's West End that it first found that audience. This was the birth of British cinema.

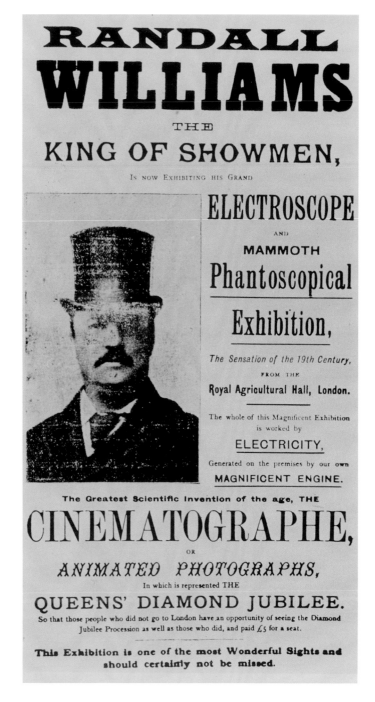

Within a few hours, films of the Jubilee were being shown throughout Britain, and soon they had reached most parts of the world. This poster advertises one such film for 'those people who did not go to London'. Queen Victoria can thus be said to have been the world's first film star.

Chapter three

London on Film

At first a scientific wonder, and then a popular form of entertainment, the cinematograph also provided a remarkable new tool for the historian.

The motion picture camera was soon recognised as a unique time machine which could record for posterity how, for example, a skilled craftsman used a tool, or what could be seen in a London street many years earlier.

Yet film itself is a highly vulnerable material. It is only through the skilled work of film archivists that such valuable evidence survives.

The effect of motion pictures is in essence created by rapidly passing hundreds of slightly differing images before the eyes. Yet it can be revealing also to 'stop the action' and study what has been captured in a single image.

This and following chapters make much use of such single-frame enlargements which have been specially made for this book.

POLITICS

For the first half of the twentieth century, film alone provided a motion picture record of the world. From the 1950s the eyewitness reporting of world events increasingly became the province of television. Yet the films made during this turbulent century reflect powerfully a hundred years of changing ideas and attitudes.

The Great East End Anarchists Battle
(3 January 1911)
In 1911 the Sidney Street Siege of an anarchist gang reinforced the widespread belief that the East End was both mysterious and threatening.

Left: *Trafalgar Square Riot* (10 August 1913)
A suffragette under police arrest is
led away from a riot in Trafalgar Square
before jeering bystanders.

Below: *The Peaceful Years* (1948)
Living reminders of the tragedy of war
parade through the streets in 1919.

Right: *The Peaceful Years* (1948)
Soldiers were called out to guard all transport
routes into London during the days of the
General Strike in May 1926.

Right: *The Peaceful Years* (1948)
Sir Oswald Mosley smiles confidently as he prepares to address thousands of his 'Black Shirt' supporters.

Below: *March to Aldermaston* (1959)
Trafalgar Square, again the focus of a popular national demonstration. Leading anti-nuclear campaigners prepare to march to the Aldermaston atomic research plant.

Far right: *The Peaceful Years* (1948)
Two new arrivals disembark at the docks. In the 1930s a rising tide of refugees escaping from Fascist Germany arrived in London.

The Peaceful Years (1948)
Sir Oswald Mosley is saluted by fascists from
all over London at a meeting in Whitechapel
in 1935.

TIME FOR CHANGE

To continue to live, great cities must constantly renew themselves. By the beginning of this century, London, still the largest city in the world, showed many signs of decay, with thousands living in appalling poverty and squalor.

As the century has progressed, the look of London has altered substantially. Suburban estates have spread ever wider around the edges of the city. Roads, bridges and then airports have been constructed to accommodate an unprecedented expansion of both public and private transport. The damage wrought by the Second World War, the coming of new materials and, above all, new ideas have hastened the revolution that has changed the appearance of London.

Above: *Hoxton ... Saturday July 3rd, Britannia Theatre* (1920)
This panorama (of Pitfield Street, Hoxton), captures a characteristic moment of busy east London streetlife at the turn of the century.

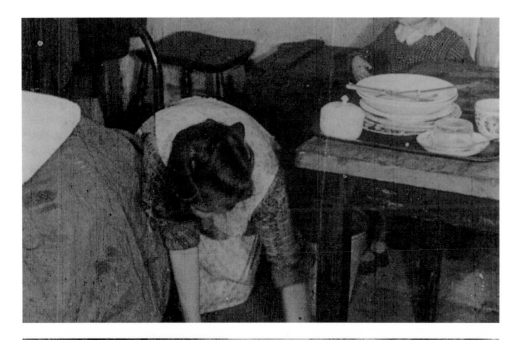

Above left: *Kensington Calling* (1935)
Although most documentaries had a limited circulation, film revelations of the circumstances in which many people lived were influential.

Below left: *The Londoners* (1939)
In many districts of London the street was both thoroughfare and playground.

Far left, left and below:

Housing Problems (1935)

By the mid-1930s, large areas of London, hurriedly constructed to house the working population a century or more before, had decayed beyond repair. It was the work of socially-concerned photographers and filmmakers that most dramatically revealed living conditions in the slums.

Below: *Housing Problems* (1935)
Where money was available, municipal rehousing schemes were often an opportunity for introducing new ideas in planning and construction, bringing dramatic improvements in living conditions.

Above: *Homes For All* (**This Modern Age Series No. 1**) (1947)
A growing awareness of the appalling conditions existing in many inner-city areas prompted the government and some local authorities to initiate slum clearance programmes.

Left: *Homes For All* (**This Modern Age Series No. 1**) (1947)
During the inter-war years much of the countryside around London disappeared under unimaginative, rapidly constructed housing schemes.

Right: *Brief City* (1951)
For a few exciting months during the Festival of Britain, the future came to the South Bank. Londoners could explore a world of new ideas housed in the dramatic 'Dome of Discovery'.

WAR

During the 1940s British cinema played its most heroic role. Of all the forms of historical record then available, sound film was perhaps the most effective in capturing the cataclysmic destruction wrought by the bombing of London during the Second World War. Long-familiar features of the city lay smashed or overturned, the objects of everyday life thrown into surreal juxtaposition.

Right: *London Can Take It* (1940)
Newsreel and documentary filmmakers, often working in great danger, recorded the immediate experience of London at war. Filming the devastation wrought by bombing sometimes produced unforgettably stark and telling images.

Left: *Homes For All* (This Modern Age Series No. I) (1947)
After the war, thousands of prefabricated houses were installed. As here in Docklands, many were on the site of homes destroyed by bombing.

Below left: *London Scene* (1954)
The area north of London Wall in 1954. Nature quickly began to reclaim huge areas of the bomb-damaged City.

Below: *City Of Progress* (1941)
During the Munich crisis in 1938 the metal units of Anderson shelters were delivered widely throughout London.

Above: *A Fish Called Wanda* (1988)
From a Thames-side apartment window Kevin Kline assists John Cleese to see things differently. In the 1980s reaction against wholesale demolition of old industrial buildings prompted their conservation and reuse.

Top right: *Sparrows Can't Sing* (1962)
Feature films form an equally important part of the record of London's changing appearance. Here East End mum (Barbara Windsor) compares figures with a bronze by Henry Moore, in front of a typical example of London's post-war rehousing.

Right: *High Hopes* (1988)
Philip Davis parks near the Lloyds building – one of many new structures that, within a decade, have revolutionised the architectural character of the City.

ON THE MOVE

Trains arriving in stations and the endless bustle of traffic in the street were among the first subjects with which pioneer filmmakers delighted their audiences.

In a great commercial and industrial city such as London, most of the population travel to and from work. In attempting to represent the characteristics of city life, filmmakers have inevitably recorded much of the daily business of coming and going.

Below: *Horse-Drawn Traffic Viewed from an Elevated Position* (1898)
At the turn of the century London street traffic was almost entirely horse-drawn. This horse tram was filmed near King's Cross Station.

Below: *The Londoners* (1939)
Trams pass on the incline leading down to the tunnel that ran below Kingsway.

Bottom: *The Peaceful Years* (1948)
An express train departs from Paddington Station in the 1920s, a scene hardly changed until the end of the steam era in the 1960s.

Below: *Bank Holiday* (1938)
Frames from a 'pan' shot showing
the crowds of holiday-makers that
characteristically besieged Waterloo
Station at weekends during the 1930s.

Left: *Performance* (1970)
James Fox appears to have unusually little difficulty catching a cab beneath Brunel's magnificent station roof at Paddington.

Under Night Streets (1958)

Gangers relaying the track of the Underground

at night. Typical of a documentary film's value

in revealing normally unseen aspects of

London life.

Underground (1928)

A shop girl on an escalator (Elissa Landi)

chats with a passing Underground porter

(Brian Aherne).

Above: *Barging Through London* (c.1924)
In the 1920s horsedrawn barges were still common on the Grand Union Canal. Here coal is being carried from Limehouse to Paddington Basin.

Above right: *Seven Days to Noon* (1950).

Below right: *The Long Good Friday* (1979)
Two feature films illustrating the decline in London's river traffic. In 1950 the Royal Docks were filled with shipping from every corner of the globe, seeming to confirm London's position as 'warehouse of the world'. Thirty years later, two East End gangsters (Bob Hoskins and Dave King) walk through a derelict Dockland, discussing potential property deals.

Left: *The Lavender Hill Mob* (1951) Holland and Pendlebury (Alec Guinness and Stanley Holloway) were filmed at London Airport making their getaway to Paris by converted Dakota airliner.

A study of feature films reveals many long-vanished types of street vehicles. Shown here is a street milkman's 'float', a removal undertaker's pantechnicon and a horse-drawn coal wagon.

Bottom left: *Squibs Wins the Calcutta Sweep* (1922).

Bottom middle: *Gaslight* (1940).

Bottom right: *The Passing of the Third Floor Back* (1935).

Chapter four

Londoners

In literature and on the stage Londoners have
generally been portrayed with distinct
characteristics of both appearance and speech.
With the arrival of the cinema, character
actors and actresses specialising in portraying
London 'types' were in regular demand.

SOCIAL CONTRASTS

At the London film studios the life of the city
was generally presented as a backdrop to
fictional, romantic entertainment; while it was
the factual and so-called 'documentary' films
which sought to reveal how London's
population actually lived. However, today many
of the finest feature films explore the harsh
realities of urban life.

Dinner At The Ritz (1937)
**Typical of the commercial cinema's
preoccupation with a fantasy world
of West End glamour and elegance.
Romney Brent eavesdrops on a
conversation between French actress
Annabella and David Niven.**

Above: *A Cry From The Streets* (1958)
Three 'problem children' await the social
worker's verdict. A feature film that reflected
sympathetically the lives of the
underprivileged.

Bottom right: *Flame In The Streets* (1961)
Post-war racial tensions were reflected in a
number of films, with varying success and
sensitivity.

Top left: *The Long Arm* (1956)
A typical 'Ealing' family. The Police Inspector (Jack Hawkins) checks a point with his son before leaving for the City.

Above: *Young And Innocent* (1937)
Christmas in the outer suburbs. A master of screen suspense, London-born director Alfred Hitchcock also had a sharp eye for the comedy of English manners.

A Hard Day's Night (1964)

'I fought the war for your sort!' 'I bet you're
sorry you won'. A revealing moment of
confrontation between generations.
(Richard Vernon and John Lennon.)

Above: *Quadrophenia* (1979)

A re-enactment of one of the violent, almost ritualistic, battles between London 'mods' and 'rockers' that regularly erupted at south coast resorts.

Top right: *Pressure* (1975)

Increasingly, feature films have recorded changes in the population and character of London.

Middle right: *Naked* (1993)

Homeless Johnny from Manchester (David Thewlis) reflecting a bleak but recognisable view of the realities of contemporary life for many in London.

Bottom right: *My Beautiful Laundrette* (1985)

A moment from a film which explored racial and sexual tensions in south London.

WORK AND PLAY

The business of keeping their city going and earning its living has involved Londoners in thousands of different trades and professions. But when it had time to spare, each generation has shown a similar enthusiasm for finding new ways to enjoy itself. Theatres, pleasure gardens, circuses and music halls preceded 'going to the pictures' as ways of spending an evening out. Reflecting the changes in work and play, film has preserved many fascinating glimpses of now-vanished working skills and forms of entertainment.

A Visit To Earl's Court (1911)
Visitors to the great Earl's Court exhibition ground in 1910 thunder downhill on the mechanical horseracing track.

Left: *The Fourth Estate: A Film Of A British Newspaper* (1940)
The annual Eton and Harrow cricket match at Lords. The film camera penetrated virtually every corner of English life and recorded its rites and rituals.

Below left: *Enough To Eat* (1936)
Equally popular London fixtures were the street cricket matches, like the one recorded here in East London.

Below: *The University Boat Race* (1899)
One of London's earliest sporting events captured on film, the Boat Race of 1899, filmed near Hammersmith Bridge.

Above right: *Through Three Reigns* (1922)
An Edwardian Ladies formation cycling team.
The bicycle – a symbol of female emancipation
– is here disciplined in the service of the
performing arts.

Below right: *1908 Olympics; Marathon* (1908)
Crowds at the White City Stadium for the
Olympic Games of 1908 watched the Italian,
Dorando Pietri, arriving at the finishing line of
the Marathon.

Far right: *The Peaceful Years* (1948)
The first Cup Final held at Wembley in 1923.
Crowds were moved off the pitch largely by
the efforts of a single mounted policeman.

Right: *Expresso Bongo* (1959)
Laurence Harvey jives in Soho in one of the
first British films to reflect the revolution in
popular music.

Below: *Sid and Nancy* (1986)
A distinct change of scene. Gary Oldman
as Sid Vicious recreates the life and style of
one of the leading figures of punk rock.

Waters of Time (1951)
Dockwork in London was always largely a
matter of manpower. Here a docker, armed
with his characteristic hook, manhandles sacks
offloaded from a nearby ship.

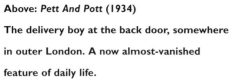

Above: *Pett And Pott* (1934)

The delivery boy at the back door, somewhere in outer London. A now almost-vanished feature of daily life.

Above right: *Bank Holiday* (1938)

Factory workers clock off for their holiday weekend at noon on Saturday.

Right: *Some Activities Of Bermondsey Borough Council* (1931)

As a horsedrawn coal cart trundles past, Bermondsey dustmen fill the hoppers of their new petrol-driven lorry.

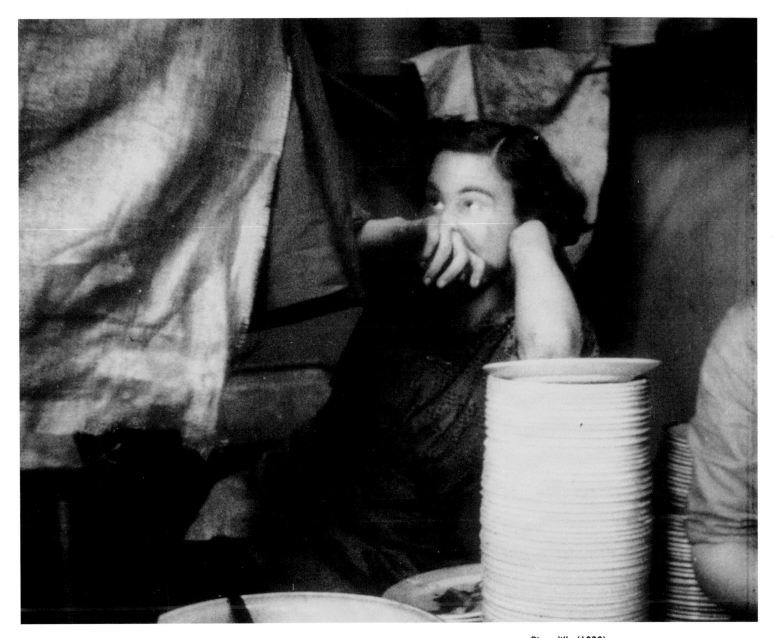

Piccadilly (1929)

A hotel restaurant 'slavey' pauses from

an endless round of washing-up.

Taxi for Two (1929)

A London working woman. Mabel Poulton

as a shop assistant in the hosiery department

at Selfridges.

Above left: *Kensington Calling* (1935)
A Kensington coffin-maker tenderly applies
his skill.

Top: *Bank Holiday* (1938)
A now-vanished feature of most London
offices; the typing pool, where could be found
the massed ranks of Remington and Imperial
typewriters.

Bottom left: *Every Day Except Christmas* (1957)
'Old Alice', last of the women porters in
Covent Garden Market, pushes her
barrowload of flowers.

THE STREET, THE MARKET, THE CLUB AND THE PUB

A London newspaper used to claim 'all human life is here'. This was even more true of London's streets and markets. Inevitably, filmmakers have found a rich variety of subject and setting there, and in the surrounding pubs and cafés. In Covent Garden Market, for example, where Hogarth and Dickens led, Lindsay Anderson and Alfred Hitchcock have followed, each adding to the rich documentation of this historic locality. Filming in a club, public bar, teashop or 'caff' has often confirmed a film's London authenticity.

Londres (1908)
A boy drinks water from a chained cup, once a feature of the Eros fountain in Piccadilly Circus, memorial to Lord Shaftesbury.

Above: *The Frog* (1937)
Dominoes were once provided as a pastime in many teashops. Here a plain-clothes policeman (Gordon Harker) pauses to eye a suspect.

Above left: *Metropole Midnight Follies* (1925)
After a West End show a fashionable way to end the evening was a visit to a cabaret, where champagne and laughter flowed freely.

Left: *East is East* (1916)
In an East End dining room Bert (Henry Edwards) gazes wistfully at Viccy (American actress Florence Turner) as she negotiates a fish supper.

Petticoat Lane (1903)

Mass-produced trousers were the stock-in-trade

of this stall-holder in Petticoat Lane – the

popular market street of the Jewish East End.

Left: *So This Is London* (1933)
A Pimlico vendor delves deeply into his cart for a scoop of ice cream, eagerly watched by his juvenile clientele.

Bottom left: *So This Is London* (1936)
This woman, who earned a living sieving and grading peas, is representative of the many small trades once found around Covent Garden Market.

Above: *Tiger In The Smoke* (1956)
Market lamps flare in the fog in this studio recreation of a west London street market.

Far left: *Up The Junction* (1967)
Chelsea girl (Suzie Kendall) who comes to live
and work 'up the Junction' in Clapham buys
fruit and vegetables from a market trader.

Above left: *Underground* (1928)
The worldly-wise barmaid has a special
place in the life of London, in reality as
well as on screen.

Left: *London's Free Shows* (1924)
Street entertainers such as this paper
tearing busker were once a familiar
feature of London life.

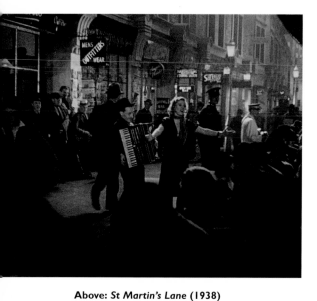

Above: *St Martin's Lane* (1938)

Another archetypal London character is the busker, who continues the centuries-old tradition of strolling players performing in the city streets. On a set representing St Martin's Court, buskers perform to the theatre 'galleryites' waiting on their stools.

Above right: *Look Back In Anger* (1959)

Jimmy Porter (Richard Burton), a market stall-holder, eats at his local 'caff' with his wife and friends (Mary Ure, Claire Bloom and Gary Raymond).

Right: *21 Days* (1937)

The Lyons teashop 'Nippy' waitress was a London institution for over half a century. Here Vivien Leigh and Laurence Olivier give their orders for lunch.

The Optimists of Nine Elms (1973)
A strong autobiographical element
characterised Peter Sellers' portrayal of
an old busker.

THE CHILD ALONE

The child or young person alone in a great city has been a recurring theme in art and literature. The cinema, especially effective in helping us share directly in an experience, has often explored this subject in relation to London.

Above: *The Knack ... And How To Get It* (1965)
Emerging from the Underground, a young girl from the North (Rita Tushingham), seeking a new and exciting life, has her first look at London.

Right: *The Fallen Idol* (1948)
Fleeing from the scene of a suspected murder, a boy (Bobby Henrey) runs terrified through London's empty night streets.

Left: *No Place For Jennifer* (1949)
This moment from the film, contrasting the great size of city buildings with the fragility of the lonely child (Janette Scott), also provides a record of a famous vanished landmark.

POP HEROES AS VILLAINS

Intriguingly, a number of rock stars and musicians have taken lead roles in screen biographies of noted London underworld characters.

Right: *Buster* (1988)

Phil Collins was cast as 'Buster' Edwards, one of the gang known as the 'Great Train Robbers' for their daring assault on a Royal Mail train in 1963.

Below: *Where's Jack?* (1969)

Tommy Steele as the eighteenth-century thief and celebrated escapee from Newgate Prison, Jack Sheppard.

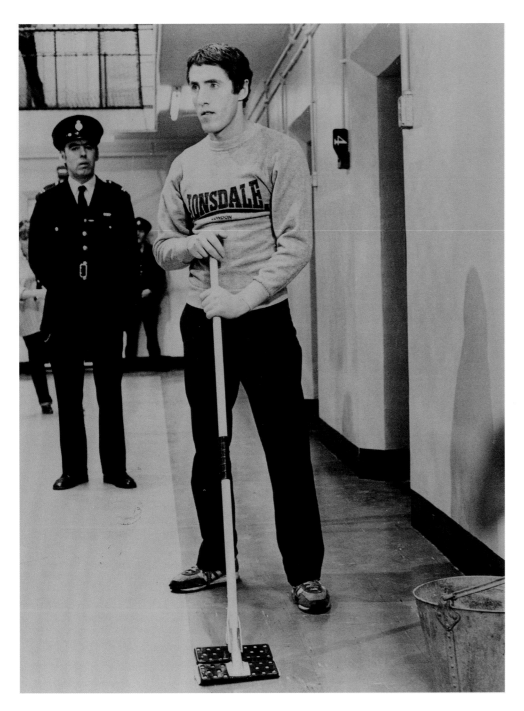

Left: *McVicar* (1980)

This film was produced by The Who, and starred one of the group, Roger Daltrey, as the formidable John McVicar, once Britain's 'most wanted man'.

Below: *The Krays* (1990)

Gary and Martin Kemp, leading performers in the group Spandau Ballet, were chillingly effective as the two most infamous East London gangsters of recent years.

Chapter five

The Story of the Studios

FLICKER ALLEY

A great deal of the accumulated film record of London was originally made for weekly newsreels. These provided cinema audiences with an up-to-date picture of events both at home and abroad. Perhaps because they were based in London, newsreels found much of their material in the life of the city.

During the pioneer years of the British film industry, the offices of the production and distribution companies were mostly located in and around Charing Cross Road, close to the larger music halls and the leading theatrical managers. Cecil Court, a narrow shop-lined passage linking Charing Cross Road with St Martin's Lane, became known as 'Flicker Alley'

because of the numerous filmmakers and distributors located there. In those days films were often purchased outright rather than rented for exhibition.

By the late 1920s many film production companies had moved their head offices into Soho and in particular along Wardour Street. This street, once associated with the sale of cheap furnishings, became synonymous with the British film industry.

Joe Rosenthal, most famous of the pioneer British newsreel cameramen, filming in Piccadilly in the 1900s.

Above: Two famous British film companies which chose well-known London buildings for their trademarks.

Left: To cover the numerous social and sporting events of a London week, Pathé News could assemble a formidable, mobile force of commentators, cameramen and recording engineers.

Charles Urban in his office. Urban originally came to London as an agent of the American inventor, Thomas Edison (whose photograph hangs behind him). He soon established his own British-based company, opening Urbanora House in Wardour Street in 1908 as a combined camera factory, film studio and distribution headquarters.

ROLL OF HONOUR

Throughout the century there have been numerous premises adapted or constructed for filmmaking in the London area. This list includes the most notable:

1896	Alhambra Theatre, Leicester Square
1898	Gaumont Company Studios, Dulwich
	Hepworth Studios, Walton-on-Thames
	from 1924: Nettlefold Studios
1899	New Southgate
1901	Cricks and Sharp, Mitchum
1904	Clarendon Studios, Croydon
1907	Ealing Studios
	from 1955: BBC Television Studios
	from 1992: BBRK Studios
	from 1995: National Film and
	Television School
1909	Hoe Street, Walthamstow
	Whipps Cross, Walthamstow
1910	Cricks and Martin Studios, Croydon
1912	Ebury Studios
1913	Bushey Studios
	from 1932: Delta Studios
	from 1959: Rayant Studios
	Cranmer Court Studios, Clapham
	Esher Studios
	Hackney Studios
	Gaumont Studios, Lime Grove,
	Shepherd's Bush
	from 1927: Gaumont-British Studios

	from 1948: BBC Television Studios
	Merton Park Studios
	Twickenham Film Studios
	Charles Urban Studio, Bushey Park
	Whetstone Studios
1914	Croydon Studios
	Isleworth Studios, Worton Hall
	Leyton Film Studios
	Neptune Studios, Borehamwood,
	Elstree
	from 1928: Blattner Studios
	from 1934: Rock Studios
	from 1937: National Studios
	from 1962: ATV Television Studios
	from 1982: BBC Elstree Centre
	Wood Street Studios, Walthamstow
	from 1916: Broadwest Studios
1915	Kew Bridge Studios
1918	Surbiton Studios
1919	Craven Park Studios, Harlesden
	Islington Studios
	Princes Studios, Kew Bridge
	Stoll Studios, Cricklewood
1920	Teddington Studios
1922	Beaconsfield Studios
1924	Southall Studios
1925	British National Studios,
	Borehamwood, Elstree
	from 1927: BIP Studios
	from 1933: ABPC Studios
	from 1968: EMI Studios
	from 1970: EMI-MGM Elstree Studios

	from 1979: Thorn-EMI Elstree Studios
	from 1986: Cannon Elstree
	from 1988: Goldcrest Studios
1926	Imperial Studios, Borehamwood, Elstree
1927	Whitehall Studios, Borehamwood,
	Elstree
	from 1940: Gate Studios
1928	Welwyn Studios
	Wembley Studios
1931	Blackheath Studios
1933	Sound City Studios, Shepperton
	from 1946: British Lion Studios
	from 1958: Shepperton Studios
1935	Triumph Film Studios, Hammersmith
	from 1938: Riverside Studios
1936	Denham Studios
	Highbury Studios
	Pinewood Studios, Iver Heath
	Albany Studios, Albany Street
1937	Amalgamated Studios, Borehamwood,
	Elstree
	from 1947: MGM British Studios
1945	New Elstree Studios (Danziger
	Studios), Borehamwood, Elstree
1946	Marylebone Studios
1948	Bray Studios
1975	Rotherhithe Studios
1994	Leavesden Studios

Left: An example of a glasshouse studio: Gaumont Studios in Lime Grove, Shepherd's Bush, which opened in 1913.

Below: Kew Bridge Studios, converted from a dance hall in 1915.

A CENTURY OF STUDIOS

The appearance of London's earliest film studios reflected something of the new industry's immediate ancestry. While R W Paul's studio in New Southgate was built like an open-air theatre, others were enclosed, 'glasshouse' structures, like Hubert von Herkomer's studio at Bushey or the large studio built by the French Gaumont Company in Lime Grove, Shepherd's Bush. At first, as in the portrait-photographers' studios upon which they were modelled, daylight was the source of illumination, but increasingly, electric lamps were used.

In the search for cheap premises, all kinds of buildings were converted to studios – among them a roller skating rink, a disused power station and a dance hall. At the end of the First World War many items of military equipment were going cheap. An ex-aircraft factory at Cricklewood became the studios of Stoll Picture Productions – a branch of the entertainment empire run by Sir Oswald Stoll, who owned many music halls in London, most notably the London Coliseum. The Whitehall Studios at Elstree were fashioned out of parts originally intended for an airship hangar and at Walton-on-Thames the pioneer filmmaker Cecil Hepworth purchased three electric generators taken from captured German submarines.

In 1910, thirty-six per cent of the films shown in London cinemas came from France and twenty-five per cent from the United States. By 1926, only five per cent of British cinema programmes were home (in effect London) made, with American distributors exercising a near-monopoly control over what was shown. In order to help the British film industry survive, the Government passed a Cinematograph Films Act in 1927 known as the 'Quota Act'. It aimed to raise the quota of British films shown by annual stages until 1935, by which time twenty per cent of each cinema programme was to be British.

Throughout the 1920s, experimental sound-on-disc and sound-on-film recording systems were being developed in America and Europe, but it was not until 1927 that the first part-synchronised, part-sound-on-film production was shown to cinema audiences. This was *The Jazz Singer*, released by the Hollywood company Warner Brothers. On 27 September 1928 it opened in London at the new Piccadilly Theatre, where it created a sensation. London studios were hastily sound-proofed while throughout the country cinemas were 'wired for sound'. The age of the 'Talkies' had begun.

The combination of these two events gave encouragement to British film producers to construct larger premises. There soon arose in the outer London suburbs a number of impressive studios, the names of which are still associated with the 'golden age' of British film production. Often built in the grounds of large country mansions, their location was usually determined by access to public transport and

Above: **Alfred Hitchcock supervising the recording of dialogue for** *Blackmail* **at Elstree in 1929.** *Blackmail* **is considered to be the first British 'talkie'.**

Right: **The BIP Studios in Elstree, in 1927, was one of the 'super studios' which heralded the 'golden age' of British film production.**

industry. The rapid growth of television led to a decline in audiences. A number of the most famous studios were sold, either for demolition or for conversion to television use but recent years have seen a resurgence, mainly funded from overseas. Some studios have been rejuvenated and at Leavesden near Watford an immense new studio has joined its older counterparts. Here ambitious plans are underway to convert a vast aircraft factory and airfield into the largest studio premises in Europe.

Left: Pinewood Studios opened near Iver, Buckinghamshire in 1936. It is one of the few great British film studios still operational today.

Below: The end of an era: Denham Studios was a warehouse for twenty-seven years before finally being demolished in 1981.

convenient road and rail links to central London. It was important to ensure that, as far as possible, filming was not affected by that characteristic scourge of London – the heavily polluted 'pea soup' fog. For this reason most of these newer studios were situated to the west of London, where prevailing south-westerly winds helped to keep the studios free of the fog which hung in a pall over central and east London. In due course the names of outer London districts such as Ealing, Elstree, Pinewood, Shepperton, Denham and Twickenham became synonymous with British filmmaking.

During the Second World War, many London studios were taken over to serve as factories or food stores. Pinewood became the home not only of the Crown Film Unit, but also served as a depot for the Ministry of Food, and as the out-of-town annexe of Lloyds, the Stock Exchange and the Royal Mint. Feature film production was concentrated chiefly at Denham, Ealing, Lime Grove and Welwyn. Some studios were damaged by bombing: Denham suffered a 'hit and run' attack and part of Teddington was destroyed by a V1 'flying bomb'.

In the 1950s a major crisis beset the

Sidney Cole, Editor and Producer

Sidney Cole has been a notable figure in the British film industry for many years, both as an editor and producer, and as a doughty union negotiator and representative. Today he is perhaps most readily associated with Ealing Studios, where he worked under Basil Dean, and from 1942 onwards throughout the productive Balcon years. Sidney Cole's fascination with the movies began much earlier:

Sidney, I know you were born in Kennington in 1908, near where Chaplin lived as a boy, but was a career in the film industry a youthful ambition?
It was an unresolved one. When I first went to the movies it was always very exciting and very primitive. We used to go off to Streatham on the tram in the afternoon to see a film at the picture house there for threepence, or something like that. My first encounter with the injustice of the world was when a truculent usher came around and said 'That's enough, out!', and we said, 'But we have only just come in, we haven't seen the whole film.' 'Out!', and he shoved us out – as if we had had our threepence worth!

What happened after that?
Well I got really hooked at a later stage. When I was at the London School of Economics, in my third year, I suddenly started to realise that I was going to be out in the cruel hard world at any moment. So I had to decide what I really wanted to do – and what I really wanted to do was get into the business. Which I did by various hooks and crooks.

Was there a particular job in the movies you wanted?
No, no, it was just that it was a very exciting thing, you know, particularly for young people.

So what did you do? How did you get into the industry?
Well, fortunately the school I had been to was Westminster City, just off Victoria Street.

A master there knew Sir Oswald Stoll [Owner of Stoll Picture Productions], and sent me a letter of introduction. Oswald Stoll owned a lot of theatres, he built the Coliseum, and he had a film studio at Cricklewood. So I sent off the letter to him and about a day later I got a note from him saying 'Report to Stoll Studios at nine o'clock next Monday morning.' Which I did.

I was ushered into the managing director's office. He was also a film director, called Sinclair Hill, who was doing very well at that stage, very successful. Anyway, we shook hands, and he said 'Would you like a cigarette, would you like a coffee? I hope you are going to enjoy working with us.' I couldn't believe it, it was straight out of the movies! I was in!

I met various people like the camera crew, headed by Desmond Dickinson, who much later won an Oscar for Olivier's *Hamlet*. And also Thorold Dickinson [the director], to whom I owe an enormous debt – I was his assistant on and off for a time.

So what did they give you to do?
Well, all sorts of things. All I knew about movies was that I passionately wanted to get involved in them. The first job they gave me was reader in the scenario department, which

One of the many films Cole was subsequently involved with was *Scott of the Antarctic* (1948), filmed at Ealing Studios.

Interior of the
Main Studio at Cricklewood.

Chairman: SIR OSWALD STOLL
Managing Directors: JEFFREY BERNERD · W.S.GORDON MICHIE.

Stoll Picture Productions
LIMITED.
Capital: £400,000.

Offices: COLISEUM BUILDING.
LONDON.W.C.

Stoll Studios, Cricklewood where Sidney Cole started his career in the film industry.

week went by and the eighth week, and, finally, I sought an interview with the studio manager. He said 'If you don't like it here, you know what you can do.' I didn't press the point, and a week later I did get my raise.

So you stayed a reader?
I really started as a kind of an apprentice, and then moved on to the studio floor, running around, banging the clapper, making cups of tea for the director. Then I went into the cutting room, and then I went with Sinclair Hill to do a film. A very famous German cameraman worked on it, Gunther Krampf.

In those days there was quite a conflict between the old established cinematographers and the new intruder, which was sound. As far as cameramen like Krampf were concerned, they couldn't care less about the problems of the sound recordist, who would be trying to place his microphone so that it wouldn't cast a shadow. Krampf was most unhelpful on that front. Krampf was adamant that he was not going to change a single light – we could like it or lump it as far as he was concerned. There was a suggestion that perhaps the mic could be somehow slotted on top of the camera and Krampf said 'Absolutely not,' which meant that Hill had to change the shot.

was ridiculous, really, because I didn't know anything about how to make movies. And looking back, I think that before I met Sinclair Hill, he was saying to the studio manager 'Look, Sir Oswald has thrust this chap upon us – what the hell are we going to do?' 'Oh, we can put him in the scenario department and call him a reader. The pay is a pound a week, rising to thirty shillings after six weeks if all goes well.' I had been there six weeks and the seventh

Could you say which studios you worked in, and also which ones you liked working in?

There isn't a special one. I am particularly fond of Stoll, at Cricklewood. For the obvious reasons, but also because of many amusing episodes in the studio – it had been an aeroplane factory, and was like an enormous hangar. Hill was actually a very endearing man. You know, if he told me to sweep the floor I would say 'Yes, sir.'

When you worked for different places, did you actually change the company you worked for?

Oh yes … It wasn't until 1942 that I was on a permanent pay roll. In a way then it was only notional. We were on fifty-two weeks a year pay roll, and in fact, our employment was expressed in terms of renewable annual options, which was a great help. The nearest approach to being permanently employed was if you worked for crews.

I suppose it meant, therefore, the staff working on a particular film at a studio could be easily exploited by the management and the working conditions could be pretty terrible.

Well, they were, actually. To the management it didn't really matter, that was true, but then the ACT [Allied Cinematograph Trades union] came into it. People started realising that the old ways of working till midnight and getting half a crown supper money really weren't adequate.

I have heard many extraordinary stories of people travelling for miles and miles to get to studios to work.

There was a cameraman at BIP, at Borehamwood, Elstree – the wonderful thing about Borehamwood is that they chose to build a studio there because they got the impression that somehow it had very good weather. In fact, it was the main part of Hertfordshire that had fog. I can't remember his name, but he lived miles and miles away, on the other side of London. The fog came up and people said, 'Why don't you find somewhere to stay? Or you could sleep somewhere here.' He said, 'No, no, no.' And so off he went, in the fog, at about seven o'clock at night. There was still fog the next morning, but he was there, bright and early. Everyone said, 'How did it go, your journey?' He said, 'Oh, I just had time to get home and change, and have a cup of tea and start back again!' I think that shows not so much devotion to the studios, but more devotion to his home.

Who were the good companies to work for, or were they all pretty awful?

Well, I think as far as I was concerned, Gaumont at Shepherd's Bush and BIP at Elstree were friendly. I got on well with Walter Mycroft [producer]. But then I finally had an offer to go and work at Ealing, which then had Basil Dean in charge. And at that time I was earning six pounds a week as an editor. It wasn't too bad. I was offered ten pounds a week by Ealing, and I told Mycroft, and he said 'Have you spoken to Mr Stapleton?' and I said 'Yes,' and Stapleton said 'You are going to leave us – you can't do that!' Mycroft said 'Did he make any effort to bridge the gap?' I said 'No.' There was a complete division between Mycroft and Stapleton. So off I went to Ealing.

LIFE IN THE STUDIOS

Many of the skills brought together in a film studio derive from ancient crafts associated with the theatre, but working alongside them today are specialists in diverse and technical skills such as optics, pyrotechnics and computer technology. Supporting all this art and craft is a small army of administrative and catering staff.

Until the Second World War, studio carpenters, plasterers and electricians in particular were often unprotected by union legislation and required to work very long hours. However, filmmaking, if uncertain, was one of the better-paid industries in the London area.

Above: Film editing at MGM Studios, Elstree.

Above left: Extras queuing for work at Denham Studios in the 1930s.

Left: Music recording at Ealing Studios. Composer Ralph Vaughan Williams listens as music director Ernest Irving conducts the score for Scott Of The Antarctic (1948).

Right: Painting a set at Gaumont-British Studios, Shepherd's Bush in 1928.

Ernie Diamond, Carpenter

Ernie Diamond was born in Shepherd's Bush in 1908, and went to school in Ellerslie Road 'at the back of the QPR pitch'. He talks here of his long career as a film studio carpenter.

I left school at sixteen. My father said 'What do you want to do?' I said, 'What about your trade, Dad?' He said, 'You better go and have a chat with your uncle, he's a cabinet maker.' So I went there and asked the fellows what they were earning as apprentices – it was threepence an hour for the first year, then fourpence halfpenny, then in the third year sixpence an hour.

How did you move into films?
In May 1926 I got the sack from my uncle's cabinet makers on account of the General Strike, so I was out of work. My brother had an old Ford van and he used to go to the Stoll studios at Cricklewood to collect different pieces of furniture that the buyer had got on hire. I used to go with him as a passenger. As I was sitting out there, waiting, a chap came out and said 'Do you want a job? I hear you're a carpenter.' I said, 'No I'm not – I'm a cabinet maker!' I said, 'Hammer bruises all over the

timber and all those big nails. I only use little nails!' Anyway, he came out three times and he said 'I've got something good for you. I want you to come in and make spears.' I said, 'That sounds all right.' They were making a film called *Boadicea* at that time and I went in there and finished those spears and then we made shields out of plywood.

Do you remember where they filmed Boadicea?
It was in a field near Stanmore. There were about forty buxom girls with a big fellow, like a Japanese wrestler, with a whip – sort of a slave driver.

I bet that was memorable!
Well, being young …

Did you get a contract?
I got one and ninepence halfpenny an hour. We took home four pounds four shillings per week after tax – that was good money for a forty-eight hour week.

Did you clock on every morning?
I've always clocked on. Then you could work overtime if you wanted and not if you didn't. Sometimes you got paid double time rates for overtime working.

I remember you telling me that filming was a seasonal trade and that you got put off during the foggy months. Is that right?
Yes, that's correct.

What were the foggy months?
November, and round about Christmas … You couldn't make films. The fog got in the studio for about three months.

So the studios didn't make a film in that period?
Well, after *Boadicea* I got the sack because of the weather. So I went back to my uncle.

How did you come back to the film business?
In 1927 a telegram came from Fred Holt [master carpenter at Pinewood Studios] – he sent for me to come to the Stoll Studios. I worked on *Guns of Loos* in 1928, which was shot in the chalk pits at Grays.

You also worked on Huntingtower *with Harry Lauder, didn't you?*
Yes, that's right. We built an enormous castle in a field at Stanmore. Cricklewood's backlot was at Stanmore.

Ernie Diamond, far right

How long did you stay at Cricklewood?
Well, sometime in 1928 Cricklewood closed down. We all got the sack. So I went to Lime Grove, Shepherd's Bush and soundproofed the studios there – that was when it was still a glass house. It was for the first talkie they made there, *High Treason* (1929).

That didn't last long because they knocked it down and rebuilt it in brick. Then in 1930 you went to Fox Studios in Wembley, and then moved to Ealing under Basil Dean?
Yes, I was at Ealing from 1930 till they shut down in 1955. It was pretty new at Ealing then, they'd only just built the new stage. The first job was putting up the dressing rooms on the right hand side of the studio. Then we built the carpenters' shop and woodworking machine shop, known as 'The Mill'. On the wall of the Generator Room (we made our own electricity) they painted 'The Studio with Team Spirit' – complete with goalposts and net!

What happened when Basil Dean left and Michael Balcon took over at Ealing?
Well, we all got the sack. There was a gap between the time Dean left and Balcon took over. I went to Pinewood to make *Pygmalion* (1938) I made the big staircase in the ballroom … I had an argument with John Bryan, the art director. He designed that staircase all wrong.

It had a sweep and that never works. I said, 'You want a continuous round in there.' He said, 'Oh no, we don't want that.' Of course, when they got the handrail on it there was a bloomin' great corner sticking out! So 'Please, Ernie, do it again!' Bloomin' marvellous!

Did you go back to Ealing after the job at Pinewood? That must have been around the beginning of the war.
I went back to Ealing in charge of the night staff for a year. They sent for me. Then I was back on days and I became assistant master carpenter which I maintained right up to 1955. I used to have all the intricate jobs to do. I used to love them.

Soon after Balcon took over the war began. Were studio staff called up very quickly?
Well, they gradually got called up. In the carpenters' shop they went and went and then they closed it down. No filming. Then the governor said, 'I've got some good news and bad news for you, Ernie. Firstly, I got to give you the sack. Secondly, you've been deferred. Come back in a fortnight and black out all the studios.' So I blacked out all the windows and I got 'deferred' all through the war.

Tell me about working on San Demetrio, London *(1943) during the war. You built a set of the ship on rockers, didn't you?*

It was based on a centre bearing in the middle, and then every so often there was a big 'V' shape, made of metal – about twenty feet at the top, sloping down to one foot. Fixed to the floor was a hydraulic ram. It was all connected up. One press of the button and it all went over. The whole thing was 100 feet long – the length of the studio!

You once told me that in The Bells Go Down *(1943) a set representing a London street was set on fire inside the studio.*
Yes, that's right. Three storey buildings they were and they were all set alight. We had fireproof blankets inside the roof. The firemen there too, standing by … We had an incendiary bomb fall on the roof once – the roof caught alight. It was a George Formby film and we had to transfer the set to Wembley studios to finish it off.

After the war you worked on all the famous Ealing films: Hue and Cry *(1946),* Saraband for Dead Lovers *(1948) and so on.*
Yes, we made a staircase for *Saraband* and a three foot model of it went on exhibition at Olympia. I loved making models.

Did you always work in wood? Where did you get it from?

Timber 6 x 2s mostly. We got our supplies from the Southall Timber Company. There was no shortage in the war. It all came on the canal.

People talk about the wonderful team spirit at Ealing but when it comes down to it, were they really generous to you?

Well, we were happy in the carpenters' shop. We didn't have a bad one amongst us. We used to play canasta on the bench in the workshop at lunch time. Balcon, he didn't mix with us at all. His brother did more. But the directors always ate separately.

What was it like towards the end at Ealing when Balcon began to close it down?

When it was winding up I saw the red light, so I went to Walton in 1955 – the old Nettleford studios – and took four chippies with me. I stayed there three years and I made *Four Just Men*, *Robin Hood*, *The Buccaneers*, and *Sword of Freedom* – all series on the television. I was in charge of building scenery for all of them.

Walton was a tiny studio.

Yes, it was. They weren't soundproofed – they just stopped work when the aeroplanes went over. Boris Karloff came to Walton. I was just going on holiday and he came up to me and said, 'Thanks for a nice set, have a good

holiday,' and he gave me ten quid. I really appreciated that.

I had a call from Fred Holt at Pinewood (he was master carpenter there for years). He said, 'I've got a film if you want to come over and be Construction Manager.' So I went to Pinewood in 1958. I got forty pounds a week, which was a good wage then. Anyway, I got to Pinewood, I didn't know what I was letting myself in for – live polar bears in *Savage Innocents* (1959)!

Fred said there might be another film at Pinewood soon, but in the meantime I'd have to go back to Walton. I didn't want to do that. I spoke to Freddie Lane as I heard about this job at Granada – well, he'd already promised it to one of his boys. I thought 'OK, that's that,' but the next day the phone rang and Freddie said 'We've had a message from Manchester to say you're the man for the job.' So I went and I never looked back.

How many years did you work for Granada?

From 1958 to 1973. I was scene master, making sets for *Coronation Street*, amongst many other things.

Chapter six

London Locations

Many of the earliest films made in London were photographed in the streets. Almost at once, people began to use the new medium to tell stories and introduce dramatic action that moved from one location to another. Just as Dickens brilliantly incorporated London settings into his novels, filmmakers also realised that London contained numerous visually and historically evocative locations.

THE ART DEPARTMENT

The task of the production designer or art director is to create or choose the setting for the film. This may mean designing sets in the studio or finding or adapting locations.

Every aspect of the set, its colour, texture, the way it is lit, and every small detail of furnishing and 'dressing' needs to be considered and accurately researched. In the early years of the London film industry, many production designers and art directors were recruited from the West End theatre or the architectural profession, but some of the most imaginative came from the field of book or magazine illustration. Today, many production designers have trained at one of the special film schools, in and around London.

Above: Alfred Hitchcock filming on the streets of London for _Stagefright_ (1949).

Historical authenticity is often achieved by exact reproduction. Here the gaming room of **Brooks' Club** as it was at the end of the eighteenth century, meticulously recreated at Lime Grove Studios, Shepherd's Bush for *The Young Mr Pitt* (1942) (following page).

The French artist Gustav Doré's illustrations
to his book *London* (published in 1870) have
formed a rich source of inspiration for
generations of film designers and art directors.
Notable among them was John Bryan who
designed the 1948 film *Oliver Twist*.

Towards the end of the nineteenth century the Society for Photographing Relics of Old London was formed to record parts of London that were doomed to demolition. The resulting images have provided an invaluable source for designers both here and abroad, seeking to capture the authentic 'feel' of historic London. This photograph of the Oxford Arms Inn near St Paul's Cathedral (recorded by the Society in 1876) has been the inspiration for some notable 'London sets', including the German films *Pandora's Box (Die Büchse der Pandora)* (1928), *The Threepenny Opera (Die Dreigroschenoper)* (1931), and the 1931 American version of *Dr Jekyll and Mr Hyde* (seen here far left).

Photography is also ideally suited to record characteristic textures and surfaces. The Society's photograph Old Houses in Fore Street provided designer John Box with authentic detail for this set for the musical *Oliver!* (1968). (Note the studio lamps in the 'sky').

THE BACKLOT

When a film requires settings that are larger or more complex than can be built inside the studio stages they have to be constructed in the open air, as close to the main studio buildings as possible.

Many studios possessed 'backlots' with useful natural features such as a lake or river that were frequently incorporated into the filmed action. Some of the older studios located in built-up districts lacked such backlot facilities and rented fields or open spaces on the outskirts of London, conveniently close to a road or rail link.

Above: A housing estate now occupies much of the site of the backlot at Shepperton where Hyde Park Corner was once to be found for *An Ideal Husband* **(1947).**

Far left: This aerial view of Welwyn Studios shows the adjacent backlot partly covered by a recreation of a Belgian town square for *I Was A Spy* (1933).

Left and below: Large-scale sets are occasionally left standing at the end of a film and may be adapted and re-used. For *Perfect Strangers* (1945), made at Denham, a street was created for scenes of the London Blitz. This was re-used the same year during the filming of *Brief Encounter*.

A vast photograph of the Law Courts was erected in a rented field at Northolt to serve as a backing to scenes of the Lord Mayor's Show in Alfred Hitchcock's *Sabotage* (1936).

In recent years backlots have been established
on an even larger scale. The suburban
London street which suffered in the Blitz
in *Hope And Glory* (1987) was constructed on
a deserted airfield at Wisley.

ON LOCATION

Owing to the very high cost of set building it is often more economical to find somewhere that closely resembles what is required and adapt it. It is the job of the location finder to identify places that can be used or adapted to suit the requirements of the script. The director and production designer may also have in mind something more than simply a suitable background to the action. A great capital city with many historic locations and memorials, London has provided filmmakers with a rich source of visual symbolism and metaphor.

The location finder constantly has to update his or her knowledge of the locations that are available for filmmaking. Many keep extensive records of places which they recognise have filmic potential and which they can 'cast' as a location. According to Charles Dickens in *Pickwick Papers,* Sam Weller had a knowledge of London that was 'extensive and peculiar'. This is precisely the kind of familiarity with the city required by the designer choosing a setting.

Location filming necessitates many complex arrangements with the police, local residents and businesses before filming can begin. Many London boroughs have appointed film officers to work with film companies, to facilitate these arrangements. It may take many months of negotiation to organise to shoot one scene that lasts only a few seconds on the screen.

Love On Wheels (1932)
Director Victor Saville had to wait until the customers had gone home to film inside Selfridges for this Jack Hulbert comedy.

Left: *The Good Companions* (1933)
The characteristic paraphernalia of a film
crew on location cluttering the platform
at Willesden Junction.

Below left: *Brothers In Law* (1956)
Although camera crews filming on location
have become a comparatively familiar sight in
the streets of London, the chance of watching
the artistes at work always attracts a crowd.
(Ian Carmichael and Richard Attenborough)

Above: *The Ladykillers* (1955)
Having disrupted the lives of residents in
Frederica Street, Barnsbury for many weeks,
Ealing Studios put on a street party, hosted by
members of the cast and crew.

DRESSED FOR THE PART

In seeking appropriate locations, a production designer or location finder will be on the lookout for somewhere which might lend itself to adaptation. With the right 'make-up' it is possible to give a locality an entirely different character.

Below: *Passport to Pimlico* (1949)
Art director William Kellner found the ideal location – not in Pimlico, but across the river on a bombed site in Hercules Road, Lambeth. On a photograph of the site Kellner sketched a group of buildings to be constructed by studio technicians.

Above and right: A comparison of shots taken while work on the set was in progress and during the filming shows how some of the 'bombed buildings' are actually studio constructions.

Full Metal Jacket (1987)

With the aid of artificial palm trees and
appropriate set-dressing, derelict warehouses
in the Royal Docks became the setting for
a violent re-enactment of battle scenes in
war-torn Vietnam.

Assheton Gorton, Production Designer

Assheton Gorton trained at the Cambridge Architectural School and at the Slade. Having spent some years as an art director for ABC TV Armchair Theatre series, his first designs for the big screen were for *The Knack*, directed by Dick Lester in 1965. Since then he has been production designer for many notable films including the *The Knack* (1965), *The Bliss of Miss Blossom* (1986), *Blow-Up* (1966), *Get Carter* (1971), *The French Lieutenant's Woman* (1981), *Legend* (1985), *Revolution* (1986), *Rob Roy* (1995) and, most recently, the remake of *101 Dalmations* for Disney at Shepperton Studios.

You have been involved in a number of films which have presented a special view or idea of London. Could you tell me, for example, a bit about the choice of locations for The Knack? *Were they determined by the director or did you go finding them?*

Yes, I went finding them. But it could be very aggravating. One could spend weeks or more searching for locations in London to expedite certain gags, like certain streets, certain crossroads, or whatever it was, and you would come back and say 'I found the perfect place' only to discover the gags had just been written out and replaced with new ones. I had always worked in a studio, that was the first location film I had ever done. It was a new experience to actually work in locations, with not much preparation time, and they kept on writing gags in!

Blow-Up was much more complex, because we started looking for locations based on a treatment, and as we found the locations we took the director [Michelangelo] Antonioni around. He then wrote the script into the locations and I think that is one of the reasons it works so well. We found this park out in Woolwich, Maryon Park. A very extraordinary park with a sort of hill in the middle surrounded by big tower blocks, right on a

bend of the Thames. We also had to have somewhere that would service a scene with an antique shop on the edge of the park, and we were lucky. There was a place there that we took over and converted into an antique shop, I don't know what it was before.

But there were certain aspects of the park that weren't in the original script, like the tennis courts. As we found the locations, the script was written into the locations. In this particular case, it altered the structure of the film, because all the mime sequences at the end of that film – the tennis courts, and the mime artists picking up this imaginary ball and throwing it about – that created a theme that they then wrote back, right to the very beginning.

There was one scene where there was a gable end of a building, five or six blocks away on the horizon. Antonioni said, 'Oh, just paint that,' just to add a particular piece of colour. This was wonderful for me because, from a production point of view, you go on location in order not to do any work. Here we went on location to use it as a canvas that we could alter and add to. For instance, we must have painted half of London black to neutralise and emphasise certain shapes. Around Elephant and

**The French Lieutenant's Woman (1981)
Only the distant warehouses are genuine
in this view of Shad Thames. The columns
and the adjacent office were all created
by Assheton Gorton.**

Castle, there was this drive sequence down to
the park. There were a lot of hoardings around
because there was a lot of building work going
on, and we painted all these hoardings black
and the side of the buildings black.

*You also painted one red and one blue, I
remember.*
Well, the red one was there already, it was a
motorcycle place. The whole block was painted
red, so it fed into the film and into our hands.
It was really a question of balancing out tones
and colours, punctuations of colour. In Maryon
Park itself, right at the end of the park, we had
this wonderful mound and the tennis courts.
There was this whole row of houses, rather
anonymous and grey, and – this is a wonderful

concept, if you suggested this you would get
fired – Antonioni said 'Paint it white.' I thought
'This is a great idea!'

All those houses ...?
The whole lot! About two or three hundred
yards! We tried to get permission to paint it
white, but it was all owned by one company,
so we couldn't, because once you paint it white
you have to paint it every five years. I went
to Antonioni and said that we can't get
permission, and he said, 'Well, build them.' So
we put up scaffolding and we built the bloody
thing then painted that white! I mean, can you
imagine?

*What happened in the case of The French
Lieutenant's Woman? Was a lot of research done
to amplify the Victorian character of many of the
places where you shot?*
When you are doing research about London,
Gustav Doré's book – London is just incredible.
All the industrial and river scenes that have
been illustrated there. It seemed to me that the
power and authority of Victorian society
needed to be represented in that particular
scene.

So how did you choose the Shad Thames location?
Well, I was looking for somewhere that could
represent that enormous industrial power
and it seemed to me that I needed to find

somewhere, like some dockland, in a way inspired by Doré's illustrations. It has to be very quickly expressed, you know, maybe you have only one or two shots to do it in. I was looking all over, and even then – this was the end of the 1970s, I think – there were very few places left. There was one place where we built a pub under a bridge next to Southwark Cathedral, and the other was Shad Thames, which was completely empty.

This little side entrance to the Thames near Tower Bridge had a wonderful façade of Victorian warehouses with big steam cranes still there, all overgrown with weeds, just waiting for development. Now they are all very expensive flats. To use it properly we had to build out and build a false dock onto it. In order to take advantage of what we were creating there, I then built the office with the bow window, which more-or-less cantilevered itself over the top of the docks. When we played that scene inside, you could see all that stuff going on outside.

We couldn't get permission to deal with the warehouses on the other side. They didn't want to know, even when we offered them quite a lot of money. But over the weekend, when no one was there, we put a crash crew in and painted everything up, took all the weeds and leaves down, got the steam cranes going, put all the signs up so that it was shootable, and then we shot it. They never

knew. We got three sailing ships, rigged up our own cranes, and we had some other tugs, and we put up all this dense mass of rigging.

Would you have had a different approach if you had done it in the studio?
I think it would have been less interesting if we had done it on a stage. We would have approached it in a different way. The disciplines of a stage, and the space that you have – we wouldn't have had the intensity of reality that we got on this location.

You have worked with all sorts of directors. Do you produce a London to satisfy their individual views of it, or do you feel that you have your own view of London?
No. You are servicing an idea which is not totally your own. Obviously, therefore, you have to take notice of what the script demands and what the director may or may not want. But on the other hand, the director may want you to offer up an interpretation of London. It is like being an actor, some directors allow you to interpret the part, and others want you to be a vehicle for their own ideas.

Do you still find London stimulating?
Yes, but … that is a difficult question to answer. The London that I was discovering joyfully in the 1960s when I was working on *The Knack* and *Blow-Up*, and other films like that – I was suddenly coming across canals or places

in Chelsea where they were still using steam engines. Four or five years later they had all gone. Those elements of London were extraordinarily evocative, and that was the London I was offering up for us to film. Now that picturesque London doesn't exist. Perhaps it exists in a different way. I would have to look longer and harder to find it if I wanted that sort of London. It has just changed.

LOST LONDON I

Location filming has often recorded areas that have subsequently altered beyond recognition.

Far left: *I Believe In You* **(1952)
Norma (Joan Collins) and Hooker (Harry Fowler) enjoy a dip at the original Oasis Swimming Pool, Holborn, created from the cellars of a bomb-damaged building.**

Top left: *The Titfield Thunderbolt* **(1953)
The scene in which the citizens of Titfield decide to remove their beloved Thunderbolt from the local museum was filmed in the entrance to the now-demolished Imperial Institute in South Kensington.**

Bottom left: *The Blue Lamp* **(1949)
Shot largely around Paddington Green, this film recorded many now-vanished London landmarks, such as the old Paddington Green Police Station, a site now covered by the Westway flyover.**

Following page: *The Blue Lamp* **(1949)
All but St Augustine's Church has now disappeared from this part of Kilburn. The miles of terraced houses that once characterised the district were replaced by local authority housing in the 1960s.**

LOST LONDON II: THE BOMBED CITY

Following the Blitz of 1940–41 many square miles of devastation became a London location of which numerous filmmakers took advantage – so preserving an unrepeatable record.

Left: *Great Expectations* (1946)
A film crew at work near St Paul's Cathedral one quiet Sunday morning. By avoiding any glimpse of wartime devastation, the director, David Lean, recaptured views unseen since the early nineteenth century.

Below: *The Weapon* (1956)
Near Whitbread's Brewery and close to the site of the present Museum of London in London Wall, make-believe cowboys contemplate a fallen comrade.

Above right: *Seven Days To Noon* (1950)
**The acres of the bomb-damaged City provided
ideal hiding places. Near Moorgate soldiers
search for a suspect among the ruins.**

Below right: *1984* (1955)
**The first film adaptation of George Orwell's
prophetic novel was partly filmed at London
Wall. Ironmongers' Hall can be seen in the
distance.**

THE LOCATION AS ACTOR

Certain localities in London have regularly appeared on screen because of their distinctive 'character' or adaptability. Places that retain a strong flavour of nineteenth-century London, for example, have been increasingly hard to find, so filmmakers have frequently converged on the riverside warehouse area of Shad Thames, near Tower Bridge, and a small complex of streets immediately behind King's Cross Station. Both have played notable parts in recent British cinema.

A trackside view of the Copenhagen Tunnels near King's Cross Station, taken around 1948. A few years later the release of *The Ladykillers* (1955) ensured that this was to become one of the best-known of London locations.

Right: *The Ladykillers* (1955)
The Major (Cecil Parker) attempting to escape over the roof of 'Mrs Wilberforce's house'. A clear view of the tunnel can be seen beyond.

Below: *The Ladykillers* (1955)
A high-level view looking towards Copenhagen Bridge showing the house constructed by Ealing technicians at the end of Frederica Street.

Left: *The Elephant Man* (1980)
Suitably dressed, Shad Thames in
Southwark was often given a
nineteenth-century East End look,
as here by designer Stuart Craig.

Above: *Pool Of London* (1950)
A dramatic night view of the warehouses
in the Tooley Street district photographed
by Douglas Slocombe.

Far left: Cheney Road, near the listed and preserved gasholders behind King's Cross Station, is today probably the most visited of all London locations.

Above left: *The Ladykillers* (1955)
At an early stage in its film career Cheney Road was chosen as the setting for a dramatic bullion robbery.

Above: *Chaplin* (1992)
Designer Stuart Craig artfully masked contemporary features with a row of false house-fronts, transforming Cheney Road into the south London of Chaplin's childhood in the 1880s.

Left: *Richard III* (1995)
In a 1930s version of Shakespeare's play, Ian McKellen rides a bicycle down Cheney Road.

POINTS OF CONVERGENCE

The ebb and flow of city life continues throughout the day and night. Paths cross and then diverge as people go their different ways. Reflecting this rhythm, the Underground, for example, has provided a familiar London setting for many characteristic situations on film. Similarly the coffee stall, now a vanishing feature of London life, once provided a unique meeting place where people of all types and classes rubbed shoulders for a few moments, refreshing themselves with a drink and a sandwich. Like two familiar trademarks these settings have given a distinctive London flavour to many feature films.

Above right: *Blackmail* (1929)
Unaware that a small boy is about to remove the hat of Alfred Hitchcock (characteristically making a brief appearance in his own film) Frank (John Longden) and Alice (Anny Ondra) travel 'up west' on the Underground for an evening out.

Right: *The Gentle Gunman* (1952)
Matt (Dirk Bogarde) apprehensively joins an Underground ticket office queue.

Bulldog Jack (1935)

Not shot on location but from a film inspired by the closure of the old British Museum Station in 1933. Jack and Claude Hulbert explore a derelict and fictitious 'Bloomsbury' Station.

HAM &EGGS SARDINES SANDWICHES

Far left: *London* (1926)
A London girl (Dorothy Gish) encounters
local hostility at a coffee stall.

Above left: *St Martin's Lane* (1938)
Cockney sparrow (Vivien Leigh) exchanges
chirpy badinage with man-about-town
(Rex Harrison).

Left: *As You Like It* (1992)
Director Christine Edzard located this
modern-dress version of Shakespeare's play on
a derelict site in Rotherhithe. Audrey (Miriam
Margoyles) offers rustic wisdom to Touchstone
(Griff Rhys-Jones), overheard by Jacques
(James Fox).

BRIDGES AND THEATRES

Among many familiar features of London, its
numerous bridges and places of entertainment
have often featured as film locations. The frame
enlargements of theatres selected here show
how film has preserved glimpses of famous,
now-vanished buildings which were once a vital
part of the story of London entertainment.

Below: *Night And The City* (1950)
The deceased Harry Fabian (Richard Widmark)
is about to be consigned to the river at
Hammersmith, watched by Kristo (Herbert Lom).

Right: *Chaplin* (1992)
Putney Bridge impersonates Waterloo Bridge
as it was in the 1880s, assisted by a vintage
horse-drawn bus.

Right: *Men Are Not Gods* (1936)
Days before the great **Alhambra Theatre** in Leicester Square fell to the demolisher's pickaxe (to make way for the **Odeon Cinema**), producer Alexander Korda filmed there, filling the stalls and galleries with well-dressed extras.

Below right: *A Hard Day's Night* (1964)
The **New Theatre** in Tottenham Street opened in 1810. Its porticoed entrance later served as the stage door of the **Scala Theatre**, from which the Beatles are emerging.

Below: *Hoxton … Saturday July 3rd, Britannia Theatre* (1920)
Originally opened in the 1840s, this famous theatre, long a vital element in the life of east London, was associated with the names of Sara Lane and the Lupino and Redgrave families.

Far right: *Pool Of London* (1950)
The enchanting mid-nineteenth-century auditorium of the **Queen's Theatre, Poplar,** was one of east London's least-known delights.

Douglas Slocombe, Cameraman

Douglas Slocombe began his career as a stills photographer. His work in Danzig and Warsaw at the outbreak of the Second World War lead to documentary filmmaking for the Ministry of Information, which in turn brought work at Ealing Film Studios. There his distinguished career was to include such Ealing classics as *Hue and Cry* (1946), *Kind Hearts and Coronets* (1949) and *The Lavender Hill Mob* (1951). His more recent films include *Raiders of the Lost Ark* (1981) and its sequels. Here he recalls his beginnings at the studio on Ealing Green.

Alberto Cavalcanti [the producer and director] saw what I had been doing and he arranged, somehow, through his contracts in the Ministry of Information for me to do things for them. 'Cav' was at Ealing also, and he realised he could use some of the footage for the war films they were making at Ealing. So before I knew what was happening, I spent two years on Atlantic convoys, on destroyers, usually going out from Liverpool. Shooting stuff for the Ministry of Information, but every now and then doing stuff on the side for Ealing – things like shots of the ship, guns going off and so on.

My background has always been documentary.

Then the time came when Ealing thought as I was already there, I might as well stay. And I worked on *Went the Day Well?* (1942) doing second unit and I advised them on their German soldiers sequences.

Up until that time I had never filmed in a studio, and never seen how anybody lit a scene. I was used to photographing what exists, and that is the real difference. Documentary is photographing what exists or as near as possible to that. The big film industry is photographing what doesn't exist, the 'make

believe', and having to imagine. You are in a studio, a dark studio with lights, and a set is built and with just those four walls of the set you have to make it look spooky, or light and cheerful. You are creating a whole atmosphere.

When I first worked at Ealing, there was no time between takes. You were either lining up or you were lighting. Then you were shooting and lining up, lighting and shooting, and while you were shooting you realised that the actors had missed their marks, so you had to readjust the lights …

Ealing Studios had been built on the American pattern. Hollywood devised all these big modern studios. They had these big stages, and they decided to do everything indoors.

Was that because of sound recording?
It was partly sound recording and partly because it was much easier for them to have long scenes that could be under control in the studio. We built all our studios on the

Right: *Hue And Cry* (1946)
During the film's memorable climax, gangs of adventure-loving children converge to foil fur thieves on 'Ballard's Wharf, Wapping' – actually located in the City near Southwark Bridge.

American pattern and we also followed slavishly the American ways of also doing our exteriors inside. So even at Ealing nearly all the exteriors were still shot inside. Take a film like *Hue and Cry*, for instance, which is known for its exteriors of bombed London. Even *Hue and Cry* had its share of false exteriors which were done in the studio, based on the matching shots. Things like Covent Garden, which was at that time pretty difficult to work in. It was very hard to match what was going on there, so Covent Garden was built in the studio – even in a relatively small studio like Ealing.

Hue and Cry is an enchanting picture. T. E. B. Clarke, 'Tibby', had a wonderful imagination and came up with this story. Charlie Crichton and I were very young at that time and fairly green – this was one of our first pictures (*Painted Boats* [1945] was the very first thing we did). Anyway, on this one there was this kind of young innocence of Charles and myself and Tibby. There was the excitement of going out into blitzed London. The ruined buildings of London had been left almost untouched and we had this wonderful playground, ourselves as well as the children. They had to clamber over these incredible blitzed buildings, half-broken bridges, archways and so on.

Charles Crichton told me that he had a great fondness for that area of London, down by the river, Lower Thames Street. Of course, you went

back there for The Lavender Hill Mob. *Did you always do your location finding?*
Sometimes places were found by the art department, but mostly Charles and myself, we would wander around together and say 'Wouldn't this be wonderful? How about shooting this here?' and so on. And we climbed around and we wanted it to be safe for the kids, and sometimes we would go back and Tibby would change a scene according to something we had found. All those bombed buildings with holes in the floors – they somehow suggested all sorts of new things.

How much do you bring to a film? Do directors have a visual sense, or are most of them preoccupied with actors' performances?
The cameraman is nearly always the eye of the director. He has to be. What he puts on the screen each day is only seen the next day in the rushes. On the set, for instance, you may have a scene where someone comes into a room and it is pitch dark. You don't see anything at all apart from a tiny ray of light, and there is a complete mood of mystery. Anyone would say the set appears to be unfathomable. The arc lights are here and spot lights there – terrifically bright lights everywhere, from every direction. Nobody but the most experienced director can interpret what the result is on the screen.

The point is that directors vary in their visual

perception. Some people are great with actors, but don't want to know about the camera, hardly go anywhere near it, and leave it to the cameraman or operator to make the decisions. But other directors are very conscious of the way they would like it to look. [Steven] Spielberg, for instance, likes to set up every single thing himself, although, once again, it is still in your hands. It has to be a very close relationship, sometimes a love-hate relationship between the director and cameraman. They are very dependant on each other until the film is all over, and then the cameraman is forgotten, of course!

Do you have, or would you like to have, some kind of input with set designers?
One always does. Most set designers are very good at keeping you in touch with them – they do the usual drawings, and then they invariably ask the cameraman 'How do you like this?' For instance, 'Do you like ceilings?' In the old days, you never had ceilings, only lighting rails and lamps all the way around. One would ask for colours on the walls also – you might want light wall, dark walls. Different cameramen have different ideas about how they want things done.

Can you remember any films that used glass shots or model shots?
I will give you an example, an example of the

thinking in those days. There was a film called *Lease of Life*, (1954) with Robert Donat. There is one scene where we needed to film in a cathedral. A cathedral is an enormous size, and really an enormous lighting requirement – it would mean an awful lot of generators outside, and lights and so forth, and this was slow colour film. So we had the usual round-table conference about where to go, I think we had chosen a cathedral, and I was saying how it was going to take a couple of days, what with setting up and so forth. But it was decided that we could make it in the studio with a perspective miniature and then a foreground hanging miniature – although nobody believed that it would really work.

So it was drawn out and the set was built by Jim Morahan. There were two Morahan brothers – Tom was flamboyant and Jim was the quiet one who would be working in the background. Tom was very imaginative, but Jim was very sound and could be relied on to get every single detail right, and he did. He made this perfect cathedral interior. If it is shown on television, look out for the long shots of the cathedral – it was quite effective.

Chapter seven

Past and Future, Myth and Legend

Battle of Britain (1969)
Twenty-five years after the Blitz had
devastated them, warehouses at
St Katherine's Dock were again set alight,
this time by the special-effects men.

RECREATING THE PAST

The power of the cinema to play with time
makes it the ideal medium to return to the past
or visit the future. Cinema has inherited the
role of popular historian and teller of folktales.
But, as with every generation, views of the past
are coloured by the ideas of the times in which
we live.

British history is full of good stories – many of them involving Royal crownings and beheadings. A number of films have re-enacted these and other dramatic events in the political life of London's past. Film has also frequently followed London popular literature and drama in retelling the stories of crimes and scandals.

Lady Jane (1985)
With an added cupola or two, Dover Castle was adapted to represent the Tower of London, the setting for the execution of Lady Jane Grey in 1554.

Cromwell (1970)
King Charles (Alec Guinness) calmly prepares for death at the hands of masked executioners, before the Banqueting House in Whitehall.

Right: *The Mudlark* (1950)
Queen Victoria (Irene Dunne) acclaimed
as she drives through the London streets
(actually the riverside in front of County
Hall) during a film restaging of the
Diamond Jubilee celebrations in 1897.

Above: *10 Rillington Place* (1970)
A disturbing conjunction of fact and fiction:
Richard Attenborough, made-up and dressed
as the murderer John Christie, appears before
press photographers outside 10 Rillington
Place, the actual scene of the crimes.

Right: *Let Him Have It* (1991)
Derek Bentley (Chris Eccleston) and Chris
Craig (Paul Reynolds) on trial for the murder
of a policeman in Croydon. The film sought
to promote a reassessment of the verdict.

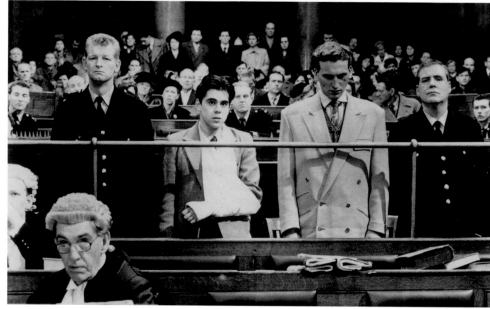

PROPHESYING THE FUTURE

As well as being able to take us back in time, film is an ideal medium to show us visions of the future. From the earliest days of the cinematograph, filmmakers recognised the power of film to give realism to fantasy. Speculating about the future has also been a way of enabling us to reflect on our concerns about the present.

The Fugitive Futurist (1924)
The Thames has been drained and converted into a railway, while Tower Bridge has become a stop on the monorail in this vision of a future London.

Right: *1984* (1955)

It was perhaps inevitable that filmmakers would attempt to realise George Orwell's grim description of a future London. This Anglo-American production was made largely amid the ruins left by wartime bombing. Their vision of the future was based on London's existing appearance, with models and process photography used to create a menacing new cityscape.

Below: *High Treason* (1929)

'London as it will be in 1940', conjectured by the director Maurice Elvey and designer Andrew Mazzei.

Left: *Things To Come* (1936)
The film adaptation of H G Wells's prophetic book foretold a devastating war that would destroy 'Everytown' (clearly based on London) in 1940. This potent cinematic vision of the future city was created by designer/director William Cameron Menzies, in collaboration with designer Vincent Korda. The film ends with two young people in the year 2036 leaving earth in a rocket to colonise a distant planet.

Below left: *A Clockwork Orange* (1971)
Forces of anarchy terrorise the inhabitants of a planner's Utopia. One of this film's many disturbing sequences filmed at Thamesmead.

Below: *The Bed Sitting Room* (1969)
A familiar London landmark all but submerged beneath a cataclysmic flood.

MYTH AND LEGEND

The history and atmosphere of London have fired the imaginations of generations of storytellers. Characters of both fact and fiction seem to haunt its streets. Cinema has in its own way done much to explore and enrich the store of London's history, folklore and make-believe, where fiction becomes a complement to fact rather than its opposite.

Top right: *Pandora's Box (Die Büchse der Pandora)* **(Germany, 1928)**
The menacing figure of 'the Ripper' has stalked the courts and alleys of many films. Here he approaches through the fog, about to end the life of the spirited Lulu (Louise Brooks). This adaptation of Wedekind's play was directed by G W Pabst and filmed in Germany.

Bottom right: *The Lodger* **(1926)**
The unsolved Whitechapel Murders of 1888 – associated with the name of 'Jack the Ripper' – continue to fascinate. Alfred Hitchcock's film on the theme opened with dramatic titles designed by McKnight Kaufer.

THE LODGER A STORY OF THE LONDON FOG—

Dr Jekyll And Mr Hyde (US, 1941)
The fog, the policeman on his beat and the familiar hansom cab all confirm that this is London. An effective evocation created in Hollywood.

Right: *Pursuit To Algiers* (US, 1945)
Sherlock Holmes, the greatest fictional London detective, has had many screen interpreters. In British actors Basil Rathbone and Nigel Bruce, Hollywood found an ideal Holmes and Watson.

Below right: *A Girl Of London* (1925)
Ian Hunter and Norah Swinburne starred in this 'thriller of London's dope dens' made at the Stoll Company's Cricklewood Studios.

Far right: *Ultus And The Secret Of The Night* (1916)
On the screen London's foreign communities were often seen as menacing and subversive. These drinking den customers bode no good for Ultus, the Avenger.

AS OTHERS SEE US

London was for centuries the world's largest and richest city. As well as admiring its great buildings, visitors also remarked on its obvious contrasts of wealth and poverty, its many separate communities and other distinctive characteristics.

Foreign filmmakers, when recreating the city in their own studios, have often emphasised those features they believed were 'typically London'.

Below: *Mary Poppins* **(US, 1964)**
The magically-endowed nanny levitates over Westminster on her way to care for her young charges in St John's Wood.

7A-3718C

Top left: *Drôle de Drame* (France, 1937)
For this stylish French comedy the settings included a number of 'typical' elements of the London scene, as seen here in a dockside street in Chinatown.

Bottom left: *Top Hat* (US, 1935)
By the 1930s the hansom cab had all but vanished from London streets, but Fred Astaire finds a survivor in which to drive Ginger Rogers across Westminster Bridge. Actually, Fred, Ginger and the cab were in Hollywood, in front of a back projection screen.

Witness for the Prosecution (US, 1957)
The Number One Court at the Old Bailey was so frequently featured in Hollywood movies that some studios kept basic units of the set ready to reassemble.

Left: *Confirm Or Deny* (US, 1941)
In this fascinating Hollywood interpretation of a wartime night on the London Underground, elegant Don Ameche and Joan Bennett join the hundreds bedding down for the night on the platform.

Below left: *Mrs Miniver* (US, 1942)
Stoically coping, Mr and Mrs Miniver (Walter Pidgeon and Greer Garson) sheltering from an air raid find solace and inspiration in a good book.

Below: *My Fair Lady* (US, 1964)
The skills of many studio craftsmen combined to create part of Covent Garden Market at the Warner Studios in Burbank, California. The resulting set, which rearranged many familiar market buildings, was nevertheless an atmospheric triumph. Here flower-seller Eliza Doolittle (Audrey Hepburn) joins fellow market workers in a cheerful 'knees-up'.

Kevin Brownlow, Director and Film Historian

Kevin Brownlow is an internationally respected filmmaker and historian, responsible not only for the epic restoration of *Napoleon* (1926), Abel Gance's silent screen masterpiece, but also, with David Gill for books, revelatory television programmes and theatrical presentations celebrating the achievements of pioneer filmmakers in Europe and Hollywood. It was, however, as an astonishingly assured and determined eighteen-year-old that he and sixteen-year-old Andrew Mollo began to film *It Happened Here*, and created one of the most remarkable British films for decades. A dramatic and chilling account of what might have happened in the 1940s if Germany had successfully invaded Britain, it had its genesis in Brownlow's wartime recollections, as he explains here.

Below: Kevin Brownlow returns to a spot where he filmed a war-devastated London thirty years earlier.

Could you say what your initial motives were in making It Happened Here?

Oh, well, the first motive was I'm sure self-glorification. It was adolescent exhibitionism, I wanted to make a sensational film. I'm sure that is all it was at the beginning. But behind that was the memory of London in the war, and the memory of walking around it with my mother ... Much of *It Happened Here* derives from that, the chief character looks a bit like her, she is actually wearing the same turban – my mother gave it to her for the film – and I can almost see myself plodding along beside her, past the air raid shelters and the bomb damage. It was, I suppose – I hate to say it in respect to that period – but it was nostalgia.

Right: *It Happened Here* (1964)
Boys mockingly goose-step past British auxiliaries of the German occupying forces. This chilling film suggests how London might have reacted to a successful German invasion in 1940.

So your walking through London is a kind of ghost story that underlies It Happened Here?

Very much so. I recall the smells, the sounds your feet would make as they passed the air raid shelters that would alter from echoing to a flat 'splodge'. It was particularly magic because I was stuck in the country and I had really no sympathy for the country at that time ... The most exciting thing for me was coming on the train back to London in the holidays and, through the gaps in the houses, seeing the first red buses. At that period they were every conceivable red you could think of, because many were from the provinces and had been sprayed with anything they could lay their hands on. There were brown Utility buses and scarlet ones. I remember that when the buses arrived at the bus stop you had to have the one with the eyes on the front ... I used honestly to think that perhaps the other ones couldn't see, I was very small. So when it came to It Happened Here, I painted them myself.

So that was the beginning. But there is this intense feeling in the film not only for the likelihood of the events you create, but also the feeling, the need, for authenticity – the uniforms and the grain of the film and so on. Is there a desire literally to be in the past?

I was always a great admirer of Erich von Stroheim [the director], but I had the English attitude to filmmaking that, frankly, if it was

cheap enough, do it. Then I met Andrew Mollo [co-writer and co-director of *It Happened Here*], and he looked at what I had filmed and he was extremely blunt. He said everything in it was incorrect, and he was not just talking about the German uniforms. I thought 'So what? This is a film, this is drama,' but then I heard the voice of Erich von Stroheim and I did admire that attitude ... So a few months later, with tremendous sorrow, I threw it all away. Keeping only the rally in Trafalgar Square, which I couldn't face recreating again.

After that Andrew guaranteed that everything that we used in the film would not just be 'authentic', not just correct, but original. He went to Dusseldorf and bought masses of German army uniforms, and ... the difference – I mean, you just have to look at the footage to realise what a difference there was as soon as you photographed it.

The locations had to be absolutely spot on too. It was bloody hard doing London in the 1960s setting it in the 1940s. There were already zebra crossings and what I call a profusion of verticals. There were more lamp standards, more Belisha Beacons, more 'No Through Roads' everywhere. Of course it would be impossible now, but even in those days it drove you mad. When you found an area which was absolutely correct, I thought it was marvellous. That old pub down in Holland Park, The Prince of Wales, which has now been

tarted up. In those days it was absolutely as it had been before the war. Once you have that attitude, something psychic comes into it ...

In the filming of that particular sequence I hardly noticed myself doing it – I was operating the camera and there was a bloke sitting on a bench. We staged a riot and I got a cutaway of this bloke sitting on the bench. He was from another era. He had the scarf, the choker, and the watch chain – he was a Victorian, an old Victorian bloke – unbelievable! And when we did the 'ghetto' of the Jews, we didn't set that up at all. We put the sign up but the hanging insulator on the telegraph pole was real, and then I just turned the camera on the street and those old men materialised as though from one's imagination.

It went to the point of getting the right vehicles and, of course, the buses. I saw a bus coming down Finchley Road – it was pre-war. They had completely disappeared, pre-war buses, and I chased it, at full Roger Bannister pace 'til I got the address off the back of it. The owner was very intrigued to be involved in the film.

What is your general feeling about film used either to prophesy the future or to recreate the past?

The ones that prophesy the future I have always found terribly unsettling because they are incredibly childish. Even the good ones like *High Treason* (1929) are straight out of comic strips, I can't honestly think of one that gives you the feeling of authenticity except, of course, *The War Game* (1966) ... But when they are dealing with the past, and once they get out of the studio (which is the besetting sin of British films) ... when they do get out on location, it is quite mesmerising what you see. You can never see it again, because often the whole area has disappeared. I feel that people are sometimes drawn to areas which have a meaning for them, which goes way back into their childhood. Not necessarily the director, because it is often the location manager or the art director or the cameraman that chooses, but it goes back to their childhood, so you see a London which has vanished.

Do you feel the historic value in film will grow because of what it contains of a past time and correspondingly diminish in terms of what one might call the fictional foreground?
Absolutely. In fact, I wrote in my last book that in a few years' time, films that show exactly the way people lived would be far more precious that the greatest flights of fantasy. *The Thief of Bagdad* (1940) will always have its place but *The Italian*, about an immigrant going to New York made in 1915, has more power for us, more fascination for us now, simply because it showed exactly the way people lived and behaved and treated each other in 1915. And it is the same with things like *The Lure of London* (1914). You could watch that for hours. The story line in it is valueless, and the interiors are ridiculous because they are set in terraced houses (which they couldn't use, because it was too constricted – so they built their own), but the moment you get out on the street ... The shot of Drury Lane – when you walk up there now it has got no atmosphere at all, but when you see what it looked like in 1914 – astonishing!

Patrick Keiller, Director

That Patrick Keiller, the writer-director of _London_ (1994) is an architect, artist and teacher might be readily guessed from the film's intense response to the city's complex physical and social character, and also to its particular mix of historical and literary associations. What is not predictable, however, is the film's distinctive form – a slow succession of arresting, often very beautiful images that explore a cityscape through which the unseen narrator (Paul Scofield) and a companion go on pilgrimages to locations that both evoke the past and reveal the present.

Here Keiller talks about the film, and his thoughts about contemporary London.

The first reason for making _London_ was logistical, in that I had previously made a number of short [topographical] films which involved going away for about a month, shooting on a journey or in a particular place – like a fisherman, say – and then coming home to spend a winter (or more) sorting out the results. That was all right, but it seemed to be a system that wouldn't last. With each film I

got nearer to home – to London … I ran out of places to go; we spent more time travelling than filming …

I wanted to make a longer film, but I didn't want to go away for six months (by now we had a child) so I thought – let's make a film about London. Firstly, we could come home every night, and I could take as long as I liked to make it. Secondly, it was about a place where I hadn't dared make a film. Making a _romantic_ film about where one lives is quite a challenge. It's easy to go somewhere else and make a romantic film – a film with landscapes and a voice-over – about, say, a journey to Rome, or to the Western Isles, but it is quite difficult to make one about where one lives: firstly, because one isn't going anywhere – there's no journey – and secondly because it is too familiar – the relationship with the subject is tedious.

London is also a difficult place in which to make images – for one thing, there are too many parked cars … whereas in an image from the 1950s or before (look at Walker Evans' pictures of London in the early 1950s), there might be only one car. We normally shot at ground level, because it usually requires an appointment to get above the pavement –

although we did do this from time to time – but the film is shot mostly at street level, so there is always a problem with clutter – street furniture, traffic lights, lamp posts, but most of all cars.

Of course, there are roads where there aren't any parked cars, but the traffic is fast … There is a feeling that is very much a result of that. It is very brutal, this continuous bombardment and threat, a continuous threat, a fear of physical damage from traffic: in the atmospheric sense from fumes, or directly, by being run over. A lot of people drive very aggressively in London, it is difficult to cross the road. If you go out with a camera you get shouted at, or people blow their horns – it's quite nerve wracking.

Why did you do it?
I thought there was something new to say. It was to do with the end of the 1980s – London didn't seem to be somewhere one wanted to avoid as much as it had been in the 1980s. Whereas before that, it had become more and more unacceptable; one felt that one had no place there. I used to shop at Sainsbury's at Nine Elms, sometimes three nights a week, and there would be large numbers of young men in

striped shirts and (even) red braces, with loud, supposedly public-school accents, spending a lot of money on their way home from the City, presumably to Wandsworth … it really was very intimidating.

Did you find them alien?
No, it was that I felt alienated …

One of the reasons for making the film was to point out that the typical experience of the city – or this city – is loneliness, or isolation. Not so much loneliness, because you can get over that, but isolation, which is in many ways its strongest quality. So there is a paradox, in that it is a city, yet everyone is experiencing isolation. How can this be? It's very interesting – it's true that London is a very isolating city, and anyone who says it isn't is probably in a rather privileged position. There are some people who say it isn't isolating because they are not isolated. Because there are groups in British society where you are not isolated – obviously, the ones who run it …

Do you find London stimulating for producing arresting images?
No, this is one of the reasons I made the film – it was a challenge. It struck me that one of the reasons for going elsewhere to make films, apart from being an outsider, was that London was visually impoverished as a city. It is certainly spatially impoverished. If you are

interested in architectural cinematography, then in the general sense London is not promising. It is not a good subject, it is difficult.

Have you any explanations for that?
Well, I think that the tradition of building … except at rare and well-known sites … is not one of set-piece development. It is very fragmentary. It has probably been so since the big expansion in the nineteenth century. Visual awareness is not a priority for English society – that is the received opinion. The English attitude to the politics of appearances – look at me [gestures at room] – it's a mess and perhaps that's all right, but for a certain kind of picture it is difficult.

I suppose the whole film stems from an interest in Surrealism. One of the traditions that I try to connect myself with is the Surrealist literature of the city, most of which is French.

You don't like the look of London today. Is it your disappointment with it or is it ugly?
No, it is not so much that, although I think the things one did like about it have been damaged. When I came to London in the 1960s it was the most wonderful place. I ran away from the provinces as soon as I could to get to London. That is the tradition of the Londoner: the Londoner isn't a cockney, he or she is the person who has run away from the provinces,

or from another country. That is the whole history of nineteenth-century London, it was built out of people who were escaping from the provinces or somewhere else.

What was the quality that was lost?
Well, it's very difficult to put a finger on that, isn't it? It is not so much what was lost, but what came instead.

Is there an international polyglot quality about London now that was not there twenty years ago?
It is certainly a *more* cosmopolitan city now than in the late 1960s, when I arrived, but for me London's cosmopolitanism was always the main reason for being here. I think it is London's greatest strength – its most positive quality – especially compared to other European cities.

London went down very well in Germany, didn't it?
It was made for Berlin [the Film Festival]. It was made for export, really. I didn't make it for a local audience, and I was touched that so many people came to see it here. I couldn't believe it, but it went down so well in Berlin – or at least, a lot of people came to see it. There are a lot of people in Berlin who like London. I think they get the message that London has been or is being messed up. And they are aware that they are going through something which is ten times worse.

Roy Boulting, Director

The producer/director partnership of identical twins John and Roy Boulting was responsible for some of the most notable British films of the mid-twentieth century. They included *Pastor Hall* (1940), *Thunder Rock* (1942), *Brighton Rock* (1947), *Fame is the Spur* (1947), *Seven Days to Noon* (1950) and *I'm Alright, Jack* (1959). Here Roy Boulting reflects on filmmaking in London.

Roy, as you know, the exhibition is about London and film. What's your earliest recollection of London?

I think my very first response to London – I must have been about nine or ten at the time – was 'Gosh, it's so big!' That was in the 1920s and I recall, then, standing in Piccadilly Circus, staring across at the statue of Eros, conscious of standing not only at the centre of London, but at the very centre of the greatest empire the world has ever known. London was history. Its Houses of Parliament cradled government of the people, by and for the people. London belonged, not to its inhabitants alone, but to the whole of Britain. Whenever you looked at a map of the world and saw vast areas painted in red, that was also Britain.

Then, twenty or thirty years later, the Second World War was abruptly ended by the atom bomb – the total destruction of Hiroshima and Nagasaki. My brother John and I thought to convey the possible future significance this had for a people packed into a very small island. So the film, *Seven Days To Noon* was made as an allegory.

And for you it couldn't have been set anywhere else – London was the right symbol?

Absolutely. The story told of a professor working in an atomic research laboratory who, deeply disturbed by the implications of the work he has been doing for some years, removed a bomb from the establishment and disappeared into the blue. Shortly afterwards the Prime Minister receives a letter of warning: unless by noon in seven days' time he has announced that all nuclear research will cease, it is the professor's intention to blow up London – hence the title, *Seven Days To Noon*. As a precaution, the Prime Minister orders the evacuation of London, and we see London deserted. For this – I think, a chilling moment – we naturally chose areas of London normally swarming with people. Westminster Bridge, for example, Covent Garden, Piccadilly Circus,

Regent's Park and the Zoo. I tell you, to achieve this was quite a job.

I can imagine! What we see in the film is quite clearly not 'special effects' trickery.

Not for one single frame. I don't think I am wrong when I say, it worked. Virtually the whole film was shot on location. London was our studio. The people of London played their part, I think, wonderfully well. they took us in very good part. I must tell you, when we applied for help from Scotland Yard they turned us down flat and we did, of course, require co-operation; but we discovered that if you go to the local constabulary they are most helpful. I remember at one time – the very last scene on Westminster Bridge when 'Goldie' hears the 'All Clear' and turns and she picks up that dog of hers – that shot was taken just as the phone went from the local police. They said, 'look we have …' (this was summertime remember) '… two and a half miles of traffic being held up, now please take your shot or get out!' They were marvellous!

You and your brother began your careers very early. I first set eyes on you at Denham in the late 1940s, but you had been in many different studios

BL14-PUB83

How would you characterise Elstree? It seems to have had a strong feeling of being very much a film factory.

The principal studio at Elstree – there were four – was run by Associated British, one of the two vertical combines making films to feed their huge cinema circuits. The other was Rank at Pinewood. Both operated on factory principles which neither John nor I considered suitable for a creative medium.

As I said, I first saw you at Denham. Have you fond or strong memories of Denham as a place to work?

Yes. Denham was, next to Shepperton, our favourite studio. We worked at Denham just after the war when things were, in industrial terms, rather difficult, The unions had got completely out of hand. At the time this was accepted because the Rank Organisation – who had taken Denham over from Alexander Korda – were making so much money with their cinemas. You will remember that in those days, the cinema was, with radio, the main means of mass entertainment. Millions were going to the cinemas, sometimes twice a week. So Rank could afford to accept the demands that were

The Boulting brothers with BBC radio announcer, Frederick Allen, during the filming of *Seven days to Noon* (1950).

before that. Do you recall some of the studios you worked in with particular clarity?
You are talking now about when we started in the 1930s. All the principal film studios in England at that time were all to be found in a circle on the periphery of London – roughly about an hour's journey from centre of the capital.

I suppose Welwyn was about the furthest north. Then, as you went round there were Welwyn, Elstree, Pinewood, Denham, Beaconsfield, Ealing, Shepperton …

… Elstree had three: Associated British, British National Pictures and the BIP (British International Pictures) studio.

being made by the unions. After the war, when other means of entertainment, of escape and enjoyment, became available the attendance at the cinema moved off sharply. Indeed, by 1951, we learned that the Rank organisation had lost many, many millions.

Well, Denham was finished by 1953, and was closed.
Yes. Korda returned and took over Shepperton. Then poor old Alex retired from the scene – I think rather worn out – and we were brought in, together with Launder and Gilliat, to try and put things right. Well, happily we did, for a while.

Does a studio have a personality, and is that important? Or is it rather romantic of me to think like that?
Yes, it is very, very important. When Korda first struck gold with *The Private Life Of Henry VIII* (1933), the City of London was waiting to pour gold into his outstretched hand; and he got the Prudential to finance the creation of Denham Studios. He was the first person to have built a studio of that size in this country. The atmosphere at Denham, I must tell you, in those days, was quite magnificent. Denham and Korda both belonged to films. Korda was a film man and you could talk to him.

In your films, you obtained some really marvellous performances from actors. But we hear, from some people that British cinema has always been tied down by its close involvement with the London stage. Leading actors had it in their contracts, I believe, that they could stop work in the studio at 4.30pm and drive back to the West End in order to act on the stage in the evening. The acting quality in British films, I always thought, was a strength rather than a weakness. What do you feel?
There is no question that in histrionic terms the proximity of the studios to the capital city of the country and its theatres was the Bank of England! The talent of the London theatre was envied throughout the world. It is quite true that, in the 1920s and 1930s when talkies came in people who were working on the stage in London did have some difficulty in making the adjustment. But I don't think we had the directorial talent in those days that could effectively handle the situation. To me, London's theatres' proximity was of enormous value to filmmaking.

But film acting *is* quite separate, quite different; because you don't have to project. If you are in a theatre you simply have to project, otherwise you won't reach up to the upper circle, or to the gallery, or to the back of the stalls. In the cinema, what you have to impress upon actors from time to time – particularly the old school – is that you don't have to do anything other than feel and think. On the screen you are three and a half times life size.

Just above your head is a microphone and that microphone is recording every breath you take, let alone the words that you speak. Remember that, and concentrate!

I think you have to have a great affection and love for all the principal talents you work with – your lighting cameraman, your operator, your art director – all these people are contributing their own particular talent. If you are sensible and wise you don't try and impose, you listen. If you feel them to be wrong you have to explain why, in terms of the unity of the piece. But that is one of the jobs of making films: that you have to reconcile a large number of very special and peculiar, and marvellous, talents.

Right: *Seven Days To Noon* **(1950)**
Hurrying to join a mass exodus from London, Goldie (Olive Sloane) on a deserted Westminster Bridge attempts to hitch a lift from some departing soldiers.

List of illustrations

The Museum of London and the National Film and Television Archive would like to thank the following copyright holders. Every effort has been made to contact current copyright holders. The publishers would be pleased to make good any errors or omissions brought to our attention in future editions.

page

10 Rillington Place (1970)   144

Richard Fleischer

Columbia Pictures/Corporation Filmways

(Columbia TriStar)

1895 Derby   18

Birt Acres

1908 Olympics; Marathon   58

Pathé Freres, 1908

© *1983 Bill Cayton/The Big Fights Inc.*

1984 (1955)   122, 146

Michael Anderson

Holiday Film Productions

(Marvin J Rosenblum)

21 Days (1937)   72

Basil Dean

London Film Productions

(CTE [Carlton] Ltd)

As You Like It (1992)   131

Christine Edzard

Sands Films

(Sands Films)

Bank Holiday (1938)   44, 45, 62, 65

Carol Reed

Gainsborough Pictures

(Rank Film Distributors)

Barging Through London (c.1924)   48

(Wonderful London Series)

Harry B Parkinson, Frank Miller

(Graham-Wilcox Productions)

Battle of Britain (1969)   141

Guy Hamilton

Spitfire Productions

(United International Pictures UK)

The Bed Sitting Room (1969)   147

Richard Lester

Oscar Lewestein Productions

(United International Pictures UK)

Blackmail (1929)   84, 128

Alfred Hitchcock

British International Pictures

(Lumiere Pictures)

The Blue Lamp (1949)   119, 120

Basil Dearden

Ealing Studios

(Lumiere Pictures)

Brief City (1951)   39

Maurice Harvey, Jacques Brunius

Public Relationship Films

(sponsored by the Observer)

Brief Encounter (1945)   107

David Lean

Cineguild

(Rank Film Distributors)

Brooks' Club illustration   98

The Microcosm of London *by Rowlandson and Pugin*

(Ackerman, 1810)

Brothers In Law (1956)   111

Roy Boulting

Tudor Productions/Charter Productions

(Lumiere Pictures)

Bulldog Jack (1935)   129

Walter Forde

Gaumont-British Picture Corporation

(Rank Film Distributors)

Buster (1988)   76

David Green

Buster Films/NFH Productions

(First Independent)

Chaplin (1992)   127, 132

Richard Attenborough

Lambeth Productions for Carolco/Le Studio Canal +

(Lambeth Productions)

City Of Progress (1941)   40

John Taylor

Realist Film Unit

(British Council)

A Clockwork Orange (1971)   147

Stanley Kubrick

Polaris Productions/Hawk Films

(Warner Brothers courtesy of Stanley Kubrick)

Confirm Or Deny (US, 1941) 155

Archie L Mayo

Twentieth Century-Fox Film Corporation

(Twentieth Century-Fox Film Company)

Cromwell (1970) 143

Ken Hughes

Irving Allen/Columbia

(Columbia TriStar)

A Cry From The Streets (1958) 52

Lewis Gilbert

Film Traders

(Cavalcade Films)

Dinner At The Ritz (1937) 51

Harold Schuster

New World Pictures

(The Rohauer Collection)

Doré illustration 100

London by Gustav Doré

Blanchard and Jerrold

(Grant, 1872)

Dr Jekyll And Mr Hyde (US, 1931) 102

Rouben Mamoulian

Paramount Pictures

(United International Pictures UK)

Dr Jekyll And Mr Hyde (1941) 149

Victor Fleming

Loew's Incorporated/MGM

(United International Pictures UK)

Drôle De Drame (1937) 153

Marcel Carné

Productions Corniglion-Molinier

East is East (1916) 67

Henry Edwards

Turner Films

The Elephant Man (1980) 125

David Lynch

Brooksfilms

(Lumiere Pictures)

Enough To Eat (1936) 57

Edgar Anstey

Gas Light and Coke Company

(British Gas plc)

Every Day Except Christmas (1957) 65

Lindsay Anderson

Graphic Films for Ford

(Ford Motor Company)

Expresso Bongo (1959) 60

Val Guest

Conquest

(The Rohauer Collection)

The Fallen Idol (1948) 75

Carol Reed

London Film Productions

(Rank Film Distributors)

A Fish Called Wanda (1988) 42

Charles Crichton

Prominent Features

(United International Pictures UK)

***Flame In The Streets* (1961)**   52

Roy Baker

Somerset

(Rank Film Distributors)

***The Fourth Estate: A Film Of A British Newspaper* (1940)**   57

Paul Rotha

Realist Film Unit

***The Frog* (1937)**   67

Jack Raymond

British and Dominions

(The Rohauer Collection)

***The Fugitive Futurist: A Q-riosity by 'Q'* (1924)**   145

Gaston Quiribet

Hepworth Manufacturing Company

(Valerie Williamson)

***Full Metal Jacket* (1987)**   114

Stanley Kubrick

Warner Brothers/Natant Films

(David O'Neill)

***Gaslight* (1940)**   49

Thorold Dickinson

British National Films

(Rank Film Distributors)

***The Gentle Gunman* (1952)**   128

Basil Dearden

Ealing Studios

(Lumiere Pictures)

***A Girl Of London* (1925)**   150

Henry Edwards

Stoll Picture Productions

(Stoll Moss Theatres)

***The Good Companions* (1933)**   111

Victor Saville

Gaumont-British Picture Corporation

(Rank Film Distributors)

***The Great East End Anarchists Battle* (3 January 1911)**   27

Gaumont Graphic

(Reuters Television Limited)

***Great Expectations* (1946)**   121

David Lean

Cineguild

(Rank Film Distributors)

***A Hard Day's Night* (1964)**   54, 134

Richard Lester

Proscenium

(Apple Corporation)

High Hopes (1988)   42

Mike Leigh

Film Four/British Screen/Portman Films

(Artificial Eye)

High Treason (1929)   146

Maurice Elvey

Gaumont-British Picture Corporation

(Rank Film Distributors)

Homes For All (This Modern Age Series No.1) (1947)   38, 40

This Modern Age

(Rank Film Distributors)

Hope And Glory (1987)   109

John Boorman

Nelson Entertainment/Goldcrest/Columbia

(Columbia TriStar)

Horse-Drawn Traffic Viewed From An Elevated Position (1898)   43

Charles Goodwin Norton

Housing Problems (1935)   37, 38

Edgar Anstey, Arthur Elton

The British Commercial Gas Association

(British Gas plc)

Hoxton ... Saturday July 3rd, Britannia Theatre (1920)   34, 35, 134

Hue and Cry (1947)   137

Charles Crichton

Ealing Studios

(Lumiere Pictures)

I Believe In You (1952)   118

Basil Dearden

Ealing Studios

(Lumiere Pictures)

An Ideal Husband (1947)   106–107

Alexander Korda

London Film Productions

(CTE [Carlton] Ltd)

It Happened Here (1964)   157

Kevin Brownlow/Andrew Mollo

Rath Films

(United International Pictures UK)

I Was A Spy (1933)   106

Victor Saville

Gaumont-British Picture Corporation

(Rank Film Distributors)

Kensington Calling (1935)   36, 65

Kensington Housing Trust

Kensington Housing Trust (KHT) was established in 1926. It celebrates its seventieth anniversary in 1996.

The Knack ... And How To Get It (1965)   75

Richard Lester

Woodfall Productions

(United International Pictures UK)

The Krays (1990)   77

Peter Medak

Fugitive Features

(Polygram UK)

Lady Jane (1985)   142

Trevor Nunn

Paramount Pictures

(United International Pictures UK)

The Ladykillers (1955)   111, 123, 124, 127

Alexander MacKendrick

Ealing Studios

(Lumiere Pictures)

The Last Days Of Pompeii   14

Alexandra Palace, 1896

(Hammersmith and Fulham Local History and

Archives Centre)

The Lavender Hill Mob (1951)   49

Charles Crichton

Ealing Studios

(Lumiere Pictures)

Let Him Have It (1991)   144

Peter Medak

Vivid/Le Studio Canal+/British Screen

(First Independent)

The Lodger: A Story Of The London Fog
(1926)   148

Alfred Hitchcock

Gainsborough Pictures

(Rank Film Distributors)

London (1926)   131

Herbert Wilcox

British National

(Lumiere Pictures)

London Can Take It (1940)   40

Harry Watt, Humphrey Jennings

GPO Film Unit

(The Post Office)

The Londoners (1939)   36, 43

John Taylor

Realist Film Unit

(British Gas plc)

London's Free Shows (1924)   71

Wonderful London Series

Harry B Parkinson

(Graham-Wilcox Productions)

London Scene (1954)   40

Frank Gardner

(Central Office of Information)

Londres (France, 1908)   66

Pathé Frères

(Pathé Frères Television)

The Long Arm (1956)   53

Charles Frend

Ealing Studios

(Lumiere Pictures)

The Long Good Friday (1979)   48

John MacKenzie

Calendar Productions for Black Lion Films

(© 1981 Paragon Entertainment Corporation/Courtesy of

Handmade Films)

Look Back In Anger (1959)   72

Tony Richardson

Woodfall Productions

(Samuel Goldwyn Company)

Love On Wheels (1932)   110

Victor Saville

Gainsborough Pictures

(Rank Film Distributors)

March to Aldermaston (1959)   30

Lindsay Anderson, Karel Reisz

Volunteer Technicians for the Campaign for Nuclear

Disarmament

(Contemporary Films)

Mary Poppins (1964)   152

Robert Stevenson

Walt Disney Productions

(Buena Vista International)

McVicar (1980)   77

Tom Clegg

The Who Films

(Goldcrest Films)

Men Are Not Gods (1936)   134

Walter Reisch

London Film Productions

(CTE [Carlton] UK)

Metropole Midnight Follies (1925)   67

Harry B Parkinson

Frederick White Company

Mrs Miniver (US, 1942)

William Wyver

Loew's Incorporated Films/MGM

(United International Pictures, UK)

The Mudlark (1950)   144

Jean Negulesco

Twentieth Century Productions

(Twentieth Century-Fox Film Company)

My Beautiful Laundrette (1985)   55

Stephen Frears

Working Title/SAF/Channel Four

(Mainline Pictures)

My Fair Lady (US, 1964)   155

George Cukor

(Twentieth Century-Fox Film Company)

Night And The City (1950)   132

Jules Dassin

Twentieth Century-Fox Productions

(Twentieth Century-Fox Film Company)

Naked (1993)   55

Mike Leigh

Thin Man/Film Four/British Screen

(First Independent)

No Place For Jennifer (1949)   74

Henry Cass

Associated British Picture Corporation

(Lumiere Pictures)

Old Houses in Fore Street   104

Society for Photographing Relics of Old London

(Museum of London)

Oliver! (1968)   105

Carol Reed

Warwick/Romulus/Columbia Pictures

(Columbia TriStar)

Oliver Twist (1948)   101

David Lean

Cineguild

(Rank Film Distributors)

The Optimists of Nine Elms (1973)   73

Anthony Simmons

Cheetah/Sagittarius

(Remintek Aarons and Company)

Oxford Arms Inn (1876)   102–3

Society for Photographing Relics of Old london

(Museum of London)

Pandora's Box (Die Büsche Der Pandora) (1928)   148

G W Pabst

Nero Film

The Passing of the Third Floor Back (1935)   112

Berthold Viertel

Gaumont-British Picture Corporation

(Rank Film Distributors)

Passport to Pimlico (1949)   112

Henry Cornelius

Ealing Studios

(Lumiere Pictures)

The Peaceful Years (1948)   28, 29, 30, 32, 33, 43, 58

Peter Baylis

Associated British Pathé

(British Pathé News)

Perfect Strangers (1945)   107

Alexander Korda

London Film Productions/MGM British Studios

(United International Pictures UK)

Performance (1970)   45

Donald Cammell, Nicholas Roeg

Goodtimes Enterprises

(Warner Brothers)

Pett And Pott (1934)   62

Alberto Cavalcanti

GPO Film Unit

(The Post Office)

Petticoat Lane (1903)   68

Piccadilly (1929)   63

E A Dupont

British International Pictures

(Lumiere Pictures)

The Polytechnic, Regent Street   20

(University of Westminster)

Pool of London (1950)   125, 134

Basil Dearden

Ealing Studios

(Lumiere Pictures)

Pressure (1975)   55

Horace Ové

BFI Production Board

(BFI)

Pursuit to Algiers (US, 1945)   15

Roy William Neill

Universal

(United International Picture, UK)

Quadrophenia (1979)   55

Franc Roddam

The Who Films/Polytel

(BFI)

The Red Man Spectacle,

Earls Court (1909)   15

(Hammersmith and Fulham Local History

and Archives Cente)

Richard III (1995)   127

Richard Loncraine

First Look/Mayfair Entertainment/British Screen

(Alex Bailey/Mayfair Entertainment International)

Sabotage (1936)   108

Alfred Hitchcock

Gaumont-British Picture Corporation

(Rank Film Distributors)

Scott Of The Antartic (1948)   86, 87, 90

Charles Frend

Ealing Studios

(Lumiere Pictures)

Seven Days To Noon (1950)   48, 122, 165

Roy Boulting

Charter Films

(Lumiere Pictures)

Sid And Nancy (1986)   60

Alex Cox

Zenith Productions

(Artificial Eye)

Squibs Wins The Calcutta Sweep (1922)   49

George Pearson

(Welsh-Pearson)

So This Is London (1936)   69

National Talkies

(Guildhall School of Music and Drama)

So This Is London (1933)   69

Marion Grierson

Strand Film Company

(The British Council)

Some Activities Of Bermondsey Borough Council (1931)   62

H W Bush

Bermondsey Borough Council Health Progaganda Department

(Southwark Local Studies Library)

Sparrows Can't Sing (1962)   42

Joan Littlewood

Carthage Productions

(Lumiere Pictures)

St Martin's Lane (1938)   72, 131

Tim Whelan

Mayflower Pictures

(The Rohauer Collection)

Stage Fright (1949)   97

Alfred Hitchcock

Associated British Picture Corporation

(Warner Brothers)

Taxi for Two (1929)   64

Alexandre Esway, Denison Clift

Gainsborough Pictures

(Rank Film Distributors)

The Times (18 August 1789)   13

(The British Library Newspaper Library)

The Titfield Thunderbolt (1953)   119

Charles Crichton

Ealing Studios

(Lumiere Pictures)

Things To Come (1936)   147

William Cameron Menzies

London Film Productions

(CTE [Carlton] UK)

Through Three Reigns (1922)   58

Cecil Hepworth

Hepworth Manufacturing Company

(Valerie Williamson)

Tiger In The Smoke (1956)   69

Roy Baker

Rank Film Productions

(Rank Film Distributors)

Top Hat (1935)   153

Mark Sandrich

RKO Radio Pictures

(BFI)

Trafalgar Square Riot (10 August 1913)   28

Pathé News

(British Pathé News)

Ultus And The Secret Of The Night (1916)   151

George Pearson

(Gaumont)

Underground (1928)   46, 71

Anthony Asquith

British Instructional Films

(Lumiere Pictures)

Under Night Streets (1958)   46

Ralph Keene

British Transport Films

(London Transport Museum)

The University Boat Race (1899)   57

British Mutoscope and Biograph Company

Up The Junction (1967)   70

Peter Collinson

Collinson/Crasto Productions

(United International Picture, UK)

A Visit To Earl's Court (1911)   56

Charles Urban Trading Company

Waters Of Time (1951)   61

Basil Wright, Bill Launder

International Realist

(Museum of London in Docklands)

The Weapon (1956)   121

Val Guest

Periclean Productions

(Hal Chester)

Where's Jack? (1969)   76

James Clavell

Oakhurst Productions

(United International Picture, UK)

Witness For The Prosecution (US, 1957) 154

Billy Wilder

Theme Pictures

(United International Picture, UK)

Young And Innocent (1937)   53

Alfred Hitchcock

Gainsborough Pictures

(Rank Film Distributors)

The Young Mr Pitt (1942)   99

Carol Reed

Twentieth Century Productions

(Twentieth Century-Fox Film Company)